COURS GRADUÉ DE LANGUE ANGLAISE

QUATRIÈME PARTIE

CORRIGÉ

DU

PETIT COURS DE THÈMES

A L'USAGE DES CLASSES ÉLÉMENTAIRES

OU

TRADUCTION DES THÈMES ET ANECDOTES

Contenus dans le Cours gradué, Troisième Partie

PAR P. SADLER

Auteur du Manuel de Phrases, du Petit Cours de Versions du Petit Cours de Thèmes, de la Grammaire pratique de la langue anglaise, des Exercices anglais, etc., etc.

QUATRIÈME ÉDITION

PRIX : 1 FR.

PARIS

LIBRAIRIE FRANÇAISE ET ANGLAISE DE J.-H. TRUCHY

CH. LEROY, SUCCESSEUR

26, BOULEVARD DES ITALIENS

SADLER

COURS GRADUÉ

DE LANGUE ANGLAISE

QUATRIÈME PARTIE

CORRIGÉ

DU PETIT COURS DE THÈMES

On trouve chez le même libraire :

COURS GRADUÉ
DE LANGUE ANGLAISE
EN QUATRE PARTIES

(PREMIÈRE PARTIE)

MANUEL DE PHRASES
FRANÇAISES ET ANGLAISES

36e édition. 1 volume in-18, cartonné. Prix : 1 fr. 50

(DEUXIÈME PARTIE)

PETIT COURS DE VERSIONS

33e édition. 1 volume in-18, cartonné. Prix : 2 fr.

(TROISIÈME PARTIE)

PETIT COURS DE THÈMES

14e édition. 1 volume in-18, cartonné. Prix ; 2 fr.

(QUATRIÈME PARTIE)

CORRIGÉ DU PETIT COURS DE THÈMES

1 volume in-18, cartonné. Prix : 1 fr. 50.

Paris. — Typographie A. Hennuyer, rue Darcet, 7.

COURS GRADUÉ

DE LANGUE ANGLAISE

QUATRIÈME PARTIE

CORRIGÉ

DU

PETIT COURS DE THÈMES

A L'USAGE DES CLASSES ÉLÉMENTAIRES

OU

TRADUCTION DES THÈMES ET ANECDOTES

CONTENUS DANS

LE COURS GRADUÉ, TROISIÈME PARTIE

PAR P. SADLER

Auteur de la *Grammaire pratique*, des *Exercices anglais*,
du *Cours de Versions*, de l'*Art de la Correspondance anglaise*,
du *Manuel classique*, du *Manuel de Phrases françaises et anglaises*,
du *Petit Cours de Versions*,
du *Nouveau Dictionnaire anglais-français*, etc., etc.

PARIS

LIBRAIRIE FRANÇAISE ET ANGLAISE DE J.-H. TRUCHY

CHARLES LEROY, SUCCESSEUR

BOULEVARD DES ITALIENS, 26

1888

INTRODUCTION

Je ne crois pas pouvoir mieux faire que de répéter ici ce que j'ai déjà dit dans l'introduction au Corrigé de mon Cours de Thèmes.

Avant de commencer la traduction d'une phrase, il faudra lire en entier; car, en traduisant les mots à mesure qu'ils se présentent, on est presque sûr de faire des fautes très graves, tant il y a de différence entre la construction du français et celle de l'anglais.

La traduction que j'offre dans ce Corrigé se rapproche du français autant qu'il est possible sans tomber dans des gallicismes.

Il est souvent deux ou trois manières de tourner une phrase; on doit préférer celle qui est à la fois la plus simple et la plus naturelle.

Par des mots et des phrases mis entre parenthèses, et par des notes explicatives au bas des pages, j'ai tâché de rendre les traductions suivantes d'autant plus faciles à comprendre, et je ne saurais trop fortement recommander aux élèves de ne se servir du Corrigé que pour corriger leurs thèmes, mais jamais pour les faire, à moins qu'ils ne veuillent retarder leurs propres progrès.

PERCY SADLER.

COURS GRADUÉ, QUATRIÈME PARTIE

CORRIGÉ
DU PETIT COURS DE THÈMES

A L'USAGE DES CLASSES ÉLÉMENTAIRES

PREMIÈRE SECTION

RÈGLES ET APPLICATIONS

THÈME I

Sur l'article dit indéfini UN *ou* UNE, et l'adjectif numéral UN *ou* UNE

APPLICATION

A studious pupil (1) will make more (2) progress in a week than an idle (3) one

---

(1) On peut aussi rendre élève par *scholar*.

(2) On supprime le *de* après *plus* et *moins* quand le nom qui suit est pris dans une acception générale.

(3) Mot à mot *un paresseux un* : voyez ma Grammaire, p. 65.

would make in a month. I have an hour to do a translation of one page. We have a house at Passy, and another at Paris. New-year's (1) Day is a day of joy (*ou* a joyful day) for a child that has been good. To-day is New-year's Day, and I have already a handsome pocket-book and a silver pencil-case. And I have received a gold pen and an ivory inkstand.

Next week I shall have a holiday (*ou* a day's holiday), and I shall go on board a steam-boat from Paris to Saint-Cloud. In a year I shall go with my father to see an uncle who is at (2) London. Have you an uncle

---

(1) Pour l'apostrophe et l'*s*, signe du génitif, voyez ma Grammaire, p. 33. Voyez aussi Thème V de ce cours.

(2) Pour savoir quand il faut rendre la préposi-

in England? Yes, and an aunt, and two little cousins. I have already made a journey (1) to London, and I have been in an English school (*ou* boarding-school). Then you speak English? Yes, a little. I will tell you a story that will amuse you; it is a circumstance which happened to us in England. (Voyez deuxième section. Développement, page 102).

---

tion *à* par *to* ou par *at*, consultez ma Grammaire, pp. 151, 153, 293.

(1) On se sert du mot anglais *voyage* en parlant des longs voyages par mer.

THÈME II

Sur l'article défini LE, LA, LES.

APPLICATION

Time (1) is like money: do not lose any, and you will have enough. The time that I have lost has done (2) me more (3) harm than the money which I have spent foolishly. England and France are the two most powerful nations in Europe. Scotland and Ireland belong to England. Normandy

(1) Le mot *temps* signifiant l'état de l'atmosphère se rend par *weather*.

(2) Pour rendre le verbe *faire*, consultez ma Grammaire, p. 117.

(3) On supprime la préposition après *plus* et *moins*, quand le nom qui suit est pris dans une acception générale.

is one of the richest provinces of (1) France, and Corsica, which forms a part of that kingdom, gave birth to Napoleon. The English have possessions in the Indies. France receives much merchandise (2) from the West-India Islands.

During the war between France and England, at the beginning of the nineteenth century, West-India sugar was sold at Paris at five francs a pound. At London wine costs five or six francs a bottle. Green peas are selling to-day at twelve sous (*ou* six pence) a quart, and oysters at eight sous (*ou* four pence) a dozen. Economy is the daughter of order and assiduity. The

---

(1) La préposition *of* indique ici propriété.

(2) *Merchandise* n'a pas de pluriel en anglais.

economy of the wife and the assiduity of the husband constitute the happiness of the family. She has sprained her foot. You have hurt my arm.

Conscription.

At Lacedæmonea, in Greece, all the citizens (1), from the age of thirty years to sixty, were obliged to bear arms. At Athens, all the young men inscribed themselves in a public register, as soon as they had attained the age of eighteen years, and engaged to serve the republic. In France, the young men who have reached their twentieth year are liable to military service, and lot decides those among

---

(1) On peut, au lieu de *all the citizens*, traduire par *every citizen*, en mettant le verbe *être* au singulier.

them who are to bear arms (*ou* to serve); it is what is called conscription.

Beer.

After wine, beer was the liquor most anciently and most generally in use. Beer was the common and ordinary beverage (*ou* drink) of the greater part of Egypt; the use of it was established very anciently in Greece, and in a part of Italy; the ancient Spaniards, the Gauls, the Germans knew it also from time immemorial. This beverage is made with roasted (1) barley, water, and hops, a plant much cultivated in the northern countries,

---

(1) *Brûlé*, dans l'acception générale, se dit *burnt*, mais en parlant du café on dit *roasted;* pour les grains on peut dire aussi *kiln-dried*.

and which is sometimes called the vine of the north. In England, wine being very dear, the people (*ou* the lower classes) drink beer only. English beer is much esteemed and much sought after (much in request) in the Indies, where the English brewers send immense quantities every year.

THÈME III

DU NOM

FORMATION DU PLURIEL

APPLICATION

I live at the house N° 3, London Street. The houses at London are not so high as (1) those of Paris ; but the

---

(1) Pour les différentes manières de rendre *que*, voyez aussi ma Grammaire, p. 301.

streets are wider and cleaner. In the churches there are boxes for the poor (*ou* poor-boxes). At the wood of Boulogne, they ride on asses (*ou* donkeys). I have broken a dish and two plates. How many dishes are there (1)? I like potatoes and turnips very much. I have cut your cake in two halves (2); here is one half for you, and the other for your sister. Your sisters are better than you. There is (1) a fly in the milk. You must not torment flies. My cousins are come to see me, and they have given me three books full of pictures. I have bought a bundle of pencils and a card of steel pens.

---

(1) Pour la manière de traduire *il y a*, voyez le Thème XV, et ma Grammaire, p. 253.

(2) L'*l* ne se prononce pas entre *a* et *v*, *a* et *f* dans la même syllabe. Voyez ma Grammaire, p. 6.

Will you lend me two sheets of paper and some wafers? I have several letters to write for New-year's Day. Where are my visiting cards? They are in one of the drawers.

Books.

Among the ancients, books were formed of that fine bark (*ou* rind; *ou* peel) which is found between the wood and the external bark of trees, and which the Latins called *liber*, whence we have the French words *libraire, librairie*, and *livre* (bookseller, bookselling, book). When they were written, they formed them into rolls, which they called volumes, from the Latin word *volvere*, which signifies to roll. Before the invention of printing types, the booksellers of the University had (1) the manuscripts copied; but those books were very scarce and very dear, so that few persons had the means of procuring any of them. The word paper comes (*ou* is derived) from papyrus, the name of a plant which grows on the banks of the Nile in Egypt.

The Egyptians wrote upon pieces of the bark of papyrus, of which we see many samples in the public museums and in the collections of travellers and of antiquaries.

Modern paper is made of rags of different sorts. The dealers in paper stationed themselves formerly in the galleries and porches of the courts of

---

(1) Pour les différentes manières de traduire le verbe *faire* lorsqu'il est suivi d'un autre verbe à l'infinitif, voyez ma Grammaire, p. 118, note 1.

justice ; that is why the English have given them the name of stationers.

THÈME IV

DES GENRES DES NOMS

APPLICATION

Charlemagne, emperor of the Franks, formed a school at Aix-la-Chapelle in 817 (eight hundred and seventeen). Queen Matilda, or Maud, daughter of Malcolm, king, and of Margaret, queen of Scotland, and wife of Henry I. (the first) (1), king of England, was mother of the princess Matilda, who became an empress by marrying the emperor Henry V. (the fifth) of Germany.

---

(1) Voyez Thème VI, p. 32, note 1.

After the death of her husband she married Geoffrey Plantagenet, earl of Anjou, and gave a race of kings and queens to England. The eldest son of the king or queen of England bears the title of prince of Wales. Richard, duke of Gloucester, in 1483 (fourteen hundred and eighty-three) put to death the two princes, children of Edward IV. (the fourth).

Lady Jane Grey, daughter of the duke and duchess of Suffolk, great grand-daughter of Henry VII. (the seventh), was raised to the throne of England by the intrigues of the duke of Northumberland, to the prejudice of Mary, daughter of Henry VIII. (the eighth); but she was beheaded, in 1554 (fifteen hundred and fifty-four), at the age of seventeen years. Princess Schwartzenberg, ambassadress of Austria, was burnt in the great fire at her hotel at Paris in 1810 (1) (eighteen hundred and ten). We have, at our country house, a farmyard (*ou* poultry-yard) where there are all kinds of fowls, such as cocks and hens, turkey-cocks and turkey-hens, drakes and ducks, peacocks and peahens, geese, and even cock-pheasants and hen-pheasants. I am now reading natural history. Tell me, then, from what countries the different animals come. Yes, with pleasure : lions and lionesses are found in Africa ; tigers and tigresses are numerous in Asia ; bears and she-bears come from the

---

(1) Au bal donné en l'honneur du mariage de Napoléon avec Marie-Louise.

northern countries, and wolves and she-wolves are found in almost every country in Europe except England.

THÈME V.

Sur les relations des noms entre eux, et notamment le cas appelé *génitif* ou *possessif*.

APPLICATION

Robert's composition is in Henry's portfolio. Joseph's writing has procured him a prize. My mother's chambermaid has broken my sister's watch. The queen's horses are very fine. The emperor of Russia's palace was destroyed by fire the 30th (thirtieth) of December 1837 (eighteen hundred and thirty-seven). Mr. Lenoir's head clerk (*ou* chief clerk) has robbed him (1). They have found Mr. Lefebvre's cloak, which he had lost in coming out from Mrs. Dumont's ball.

Walter Scott's novels, like Lord Byron's poems, are translated into French. Have you read Chateaubriand's works? Yes, and Lamartine's poems. They have given me for my new-year's gift Cook's Voyages around the world. The king's library is open to the public. Your bookseller's shop is shut (*ou* closed). Have the complaisance to go into your father's study, you will find there the first volume of Madame Cottin's works ; put it with Madame de Sévigné's letters, and send them to your sister's school.

---

(1) En parlant de la personne volée, il faut em-

THÈME VI

DES NOMS DE NOMBRE

APPLICATION

I have made one journey to (1) Germany, two to Belgium, and three to England. We have bought four volumes for five or six francs. It is seven or eight leagues from Calais to Dover. The price of the passage is nine or ten francs. For eleven or twelve francs, one can go from Calais to London.

---

ployer le verbe *to rob;* mais en rapport à la chose volée il faut se servir de *to steal*, qui est irrégulier.

(1) Ici on se sert de la préposition *to*, à, parce qu'on va d'un pays à un autre; la préposition *in*, dans, donnerait à entendre que l'on fait un voyage dans le pays où l'on est déjà.

Write in English, and in full, the following numbers : three, thirteen, and thirty; four, fourteen, and forty ; five, fifteen, and fifty ; six, sixteen, and sixty ; seven, seventeen, and seventy ; eight, eighteen and eighty ; nine, nineteen, and ninety ; twenty-two, thirty-three, forty-four, fifty-five, sixty-six, seventy-seven, eighty-eight, ninety-nine, a hundred, a hundred and one, two hundred and two, three hundred and three, four hundred and four, five hundred and five, six hundred and six, seven hundred and seven, eight hundred and eight, nine hundred and nine, two hundred and twenty-two, three hundred and thirty-three, four hundred and forty-four, five hundred and fifty-five, six hundred and sixty-six, seven hundred and seventy-seven, eight hundred and eighty-eight, nine hundred and ninety-nine, a thousand (*ou* one thousand), a million (*ou* one million).

Horses.

The duration (*ou* length) of the life of a horse is from twenty-eight to thirty years. The number of horses in France was, in eighteen hundred and twenty, one million six hundred and fifty-six thousand; in England, one million eight hundred thousand; in Scotland, two hundred and forty-three thousand, in Ireland three hundred thousand; total for the British isles, two million three hundred and forty-three thousand. On (*ou* by) comparing to (*ou* with) the population of each country the number of horses it possesses, in Great Britain we find one horse to ten inhabitants; that is the number necessary for the wants of society. Prussia has reached this proportion; Austria reckons one to eleven inhabitants; Sweden one to twelve; the Low-Countries one to thirteen; in France they reckon only one to nineteen inhabitants.

Doctors and Lawyers.

An observer has made the calculation, according to the almanacks of Paris and the departments, that there exist in France one million seven hundred thousand eight hundred and forty-three doctors; and according to another calculation, which is said to be very exact, there are but one million four hundred thousand six hundred and fifty-one sick persons (*ou* patients). In another calculation there are one million nine hundred thousand four hundred and three lawyers, and the rolls (*ou* lists) show but nine hundred and ninety thousand causes to plead. If the nine hundred and ten thousand four hundred and three idle lawyers do not fall sick with grief, there are three hundred thousand one hundred and ninety-two doctors who will remain (*ou* sit) with their arms folded.

Fish eaten at London.

In a curious work upon the fisheries, we see that they eat annually at London one million nine hundred and fifty-four thousand six hundred lobsters, three million seventy-six thousand seven hundred mackerels, three million three hundred and thirty-six thousand four hundred and seven barrels (*ou* casks) of herrings, eighty-seven thousand nine hundred and fifty-eight turbots, etc., etc. In fine, the supply of the fish-market of London does not employ fewer than three thousand eight hundred and twenty-seven vessels of different sizes.

Louis XVI. (the sixteenth), king of France, was decapitated on the 21st (twenty-first) of January 1793 (seventeen hundred *ou* one thousand seven hundred and ninety-three). Charles I. (the first) of England had his head cut off at London on the 30th (thirtieth) of January 1649 (sixteen hundred and forty-nine). Henry VIII. (the eighth) reigned in England from 1509 (fifteen hundred and nine) till 1547 (fifteen hundred and forty-seven); he had six wives, two of whom, Anne Boleyn, and Catherine Howard, were beheaded; the first on the 19th (nineteenth) of May, 1536 (fifteen hundred and thirty-six), and the second on the 13th (thirteenth) of February, 1541 (fifteen hundred and forty-one). Queen Victoria ascended the throne of England at the death of her uncle, William IV. (the fourth), on the 20th (twentieth) of June, 1837 (eighteen hundred and thirty-seven). At her accession she had not yet attained the age of twenty years.

THÈME VII

DES ADJECTIFS

APPLICATION

I have a good penknife. You have some good pencils. Have you a good pen? I have some very good steel pens. When the days are long the nights are short, and when the nights are long the days are short. The day appears long to the idle. He is a studious pupil. Studious children make rapid progress. I have bought an amusing book. Walter Scott's novels are very amusing. The English language is rich. Yes, I find it richer than I thought it. Which is the richest of the modern languages? I cannot tell you. A language is poor if it does not possess enough (*ou* a sufficient number of) words to express the thoughts of those who speak it. The northern languages (*ou* the languages of the north) are less rich than those of the south of Europe. Having nothing to do is a tedious thing. Idle children are more annoying (*ou* more tiresome) than giddy ones. Great talkers are most annoying people. The French have shown themselves courageous on a thousand occasions. Hypocrisy, ingratitude, and selfishness are the most odious of vices.

THÈME VIII

DES PRONOMS PERSONNELS

APPLICATION

I thank you very much, you have rendered me a real (*ou* true) service. Will you lend me your dictionary? I have lent it to your brother, who has mislaid it. That will prevent me from giving you the translation which I promised you. You will give it to me to-morrow or the day after to-morrow, I am not in a hurry. Where is Henry? He is in the yard. Tell him to come here. My sister has told me that she would give me some new-year's gifts on New-year's Day. They hear us. We hear them. They are dressing to go with me to the ball. Have you given them what you had promised them? Call your sister. I have called her. Call her again, and tell her that we are waiting for her. Lend me your penknife. I have lost it. Put away (*ou* lock up) your things. I have put them away. Thou (1) hurtest me (*ou* you hurt me). Thou makest too much noise. I hear thee (2) and I (2) see thee.

---

(1) Dans la conversation, les Anglais ne se tutoient pas.

(2) On peut sous-entendre ces deux pronoms.

THÈME IX

DES PRONOMS OU ADJECTIFS POSSESSIFS

APPLICATION

I am going to London with my father to bring back my sister, who is at school with two of my cousins. Thy father is very good to thee, and thy mother spoils thee. Thy parents spoil thee yet more, they are more indulgent than mine. Oh! that is not true, compare my new-year's gifts with thine. Your brother has shown me his drawings; it appears that his master is satisfied with him. Yes, and his mother has promised him a handsome watch. My sister is ill, she has not the courage to occupy herself, either with her drawing or her music; she has suspended her lessons until her recovery. Look at that bird; it is making its nest. No, it has already made its nest, it is now hatching (*où* sitting on) its eggs. When a bird sleeps, it puts its head under its wing. Our maid is an English woman. Our servants are in the country, to prepare the country house for our arrival. Your country house is larger than ours. Yours is on the Loire, is it not? My cousins are going to pass their holidays at their uncle's at Dieppe. This book is mine. No, it is not thine, for it is mine. Ask your brother if this penknife is his. My sister told me that it was hers. She has lost hers, and now she wants mine. My sisters say that those dominoes are theirs, and my cousins maintain that they are theirs (*ou* that they belong to them), because they have lost theirs.

THÈME X

DES PRONOMS OU ADJECTIFS RELATIFS

APPLICATION

Who gave you that? A lady who lives at Versailles, and who often comes to see us. Is it the lady that I saw at your ball? Yes, with her husband, who is colonel (1) of a regiment that is going (2) to set off for Africa. It is the colonel with whom

---

(1) Prononcez *keurnelle*.

(2) Pour annoncer que l'on va faire quelque chose, on se sert du verbe *to be* avec le participe présent de *to go*.

I fought a duel. To whom did you speak? I spoke to a gentleman whom I found in an office; I think he is the gentleman of whom you spoke to me. And what did he say to you? He told me that he did not know whom I was talking about (*ou* speaking of).

He who has little wealth is not poor; but he who desires more, is extremely so. Anger is an unruly passion which takes arms (*ou* has recourse to arms) without waiting for the consent of reason. A pure (*ou* clear) conscience is a soft pillow, upon which one reposes tranquilly. Women are the brilliant flowers of human nature, angelic creatures, whose feebleness implores our support, whose tenderness calls forth our love, whose gentleness corrects our roughness, whose goodness inspires us with virtue. Modesty is a just moderation of the mind which restrains (*ou* curbs) the passions, and checks the sallies of self-love. Those who give advice (1) without accompanying it with examples resemble the posts that we see in the country, which point out the roads without following (*ou* travelling over) them.

THÈME XI

DES ADJECTIFS DÉMONSTRATIFS

APPLICATION

Will you lend me that book? Which, this or that? This one; but if you

(1) ***Advice***, dans le sens de conseil, se met au singulier.

want it, I will take that one. This ink is not good, give me that bottle. What do you think of (*ou* how do you like) those pens? This one is not good, take that. Look at this album and these pencils which I have received for my new-year's gift (*ou* Christmas-box). Show me those engravings (*ou* prints) of which you spoke to me. You will find them in that drawer. Yes, here they are. No, they are not these; they are my sister's, but those are mine. Where do you buy those gloves? I bought these at Paris, and those at London. These cost me three francs, and for those I paid two shillings.

THÈME XII

Sur le pronom indéfini ON.

APPLICATION

One may study at any age, but not at any age be a student. One ought to lay up in youth to enjoy in old age. We believe that hidden faults cease to be faults, and that we are innocent as long as we cannot be convicted (*ou* innocent until we are found out). It is by what people say that we can judge of the value of their silence. One repents often of having spoken, but rarely of having held one's tongue. One has time for every thing, when one knows how to economise it. One travels very quickly on the railways. Since they have made a railway from

Paris to Calais, we can go to London in less time than we formerly employed in going to Abbeville. What do they burn at London? They burn only pit coal. One cannot see the pictures (*ou* paintings) at the Louvre, because they are working there for repairs. They have reduced the prices of the places in the coaches, so that one can now go to London very cheaply. They say that the winter will be hard (*ou* severe).

THÈME XIII

Sur le pronom EN.

APPLICATION

You ask me for some pens, I have not any; if I had, I would give you some. Have you visited the public buildings of London? I have visited some of them. What do you think of them? There are some very fine ones. Do you think that there are as many as at Paris? In comparison to the extent of the two capitals, perhaps there are not so many. The streets of London are broad, and the cleanness of them is admirable. I have bought some very good pencils at London. How many of them have you? I have six or eight dozen (1). Will you sell me a dozen of them, if you have more (of them) than you want? If you will accept a dozen of them, they are at your service.

---

(1) Dans le style familier, les mots *dozen* et *pair* se mettent au singulier. Voyez ma Grammaire pratique, p. 28.

I have also brought some Irish linen, will you have any? I will take one piece with pleasure, if you have so much to dispose of (*ou* to spare). The attention that one pays to work prevents one from feeling the fatigue of it. Wit is the blossom (*ou* flower) of the imagination, judgment is the fruit. To have true friends we must be capable of making (1) and worthy of possessing them. The years of a studious man are longer than those of the generality of men, because he profits by every moment of them. Instruction is a treasure, work is the key to it. Time appears long to those only who do not know how to employ

(1) En anglais, les prépositions, à l'exception de *to*, gouvernent le participe présent du verbe qui suit.

it. You had a handsome watch, what have you done with it? I have it still, but I have broken the hands. That is a bad acquaintance, you must break it off (*ou* he is a bad acquaintance, you must separate yourself from him).

THÈME XIV

Sur Y employé comme pronom et comme adverbe.

APPLICATION

I have endeavoured to translate some verses, but I do not understand anything of them. Try, I do not oppose it. Have you answered his letter? I will not answer it. Have you found anything offensive in it? No, I have not found anything extraordinary in it. I will do it, if you wish it. I don't care much about it. In whatever country I have been, I have lived there as if I were to pass my life in it. Have you been in Switzerland? Yes, I have remained there three months; one is very comfortable there in summer. Hope often deceives us, but we have always the same confidence in it (*ou* reliance on it). To see (*ou* seeing) the object towards which we tend, is judgment; to attain (*ou* attaining) it, is correctness; stopping when we have attained it, is strength.

When we are far from our country, we feel the bonds which unite us to it. Politeness is an attentiveness to study the tastes of others and to conform to them. He who learns the rules of wisdom without regulating his life according to them, is like a man who would till his ground without sowing seed in it. He promises all that one asks him, therefore I don't rely on him. They say so much ill of that man, and I see so little in him. When people are wicked one must not confide in them. That woman is frankness itself, you may rely on her. Although I speak much of you, I think of you still more. The more we consider man, the more weakness and the more grandeur (*ou* greatness) we discover in him.

THÈME XV

Sur Y AVOIR, c'est-à-dire IL Y A, IL Y AVAIT, etc.

APPLICATION

There is a railway from Paris to St-Germain. There are eighteen departures (*ou* trains) a day. How many locomotives are there? There is one to each train; but when there are many carriages, they put two. How far is it from Paris to St-Germain. They say that it is five leagues. It is two months from now till New-year's Day. In December, 1837 (eighteen hundred and thirty-seven) there was a fire at London, the Exchange was destroyed, and nearly at (*ou* about) the same epoch (*ou* time) there were two other great fires; one at St. Petersburg, the capital of Russia, where the emperor's palace was reduced to ashes; and the other at Paris, which saw its Italian theatre become a prey to the flames.

There will be a distribution of prizes in the colleges next week. They have told me (*ou* I have been told) that there would also be a banquet. Yes, where all the scholars who have obtained nominations (*ou* whose names have been proclaimed) will be assembled. There are no people so empty as those who are full of themselves. There is little advantage in pleasing one's self, when one does not please any body else. There is no repose sweeter than that which is purchased (*ou* procured) by work. There are few people who are superior to their reputation; there are many who are inferior to it. There are no real superiorities but those of genius and virtue.

THÈME XVI

Sur IL FAUT, FALLOIR.

APPLICATION

I must go to see my sister, who is ill, as she does not rise. You must come and play with us to-morrow, it is my birthday. I thank you, but I must take my English lesson before going. It is true (*ou* you are right), you must not fail. My father says that we must speak English together. He is right, for it is necessary to speak, in order to accustom one's self to it. It is true, but we must not laugh at each other. They must have worked (*ou* studied) well, since they have each obtained (*ou* gained) a prize. Tell your sisters that they must soon come and see us. Your brother is idle, he must rise earlier.

To like any one, it is necessary to know him; in order to know, it is necessary to prove him ; one should therefore be cautious in granting one s friendship. We must be respectful to our superiors, deferential to our equals, and polite to our inferiors. We should be affable without familiarity, civil without importunity, polite without affectation. During our youth we ought, by a prudent and temperate life, to prepare for ourselves a happy old age. One must pass through (*ou* endure) pain to obtain pleasure. One must like the study of the sciences to be happy in this life. You ought to have been punished in order to make you work. You must have forgotten me, not to write to me. You should have risen at six o'clock, in order to set off at seven.

THÈME XVII

Sur DEVOIR.

APPLICATION

One single day lost ought to cause us regret. Contradiction should awaken (*ou* excite) attention, and not anger. One should listen to (*ou* hear) him who contradicts, since our cause ought always to be that of truth. A wise man should do his duty without any other motive than his duty. The weariness that accompanies idleness ought to serve as a natural warning of the necessity of working. Nothing ought to correct us more of our faults than our propensity to condemn the faults of others. One should seek to instruct one's self not to be either too timid or too bold through ignorance.

We ought to reckon our days by our good actions (*ou* deeds) only. We should be avaricious only of time. Ought we not to do our tasks? You ought to write more frequently to your relations (1). You ought not to have made me wait. He ought to

---

(1) Le mot anglais *parents* signifie père et mère; *relations* se dit pour parents en général.

have answered my letter. One always owes gratitude to one's masters (*ou* teachers). He owes more than he can pay. We owe respect to our parents. I owe you many thanks. We owe each other (*ou* to each other) mutual support.

THÈME XVIII

Sur POUVOIR et VOULOIR.

APPLICATION

Our body is a watch that the clockmaker (*ou* watchmaker), that is to say, the doctor, cannot open. He can only handle it blindfold (*ou* in the dark, *ou* by guess); therefore he frequently mistakes the disease and the remedy. One can never have too much wit, but one may sometimes show it too much. When one can do all that one wishes, it is not easy to wish only what one ought. By constancy one may surmount all difficulties (*ou* every difficulty). I was so fatigued that I could not dance any more (*ou* any longer). We shall not be able to (*ou* we cannot) set off to-morrow, because the coachmaker told us that he could not give us (*ou* let us have) our carriage until the day after to-morrow. Could you lend me your opera-glass for this evening? You could not use (*ou* make use of) it, because it is broken.

Now we may go and play, because we have finished our lessons. Ask papa if we may go to St-Germain to-morrow, by the railway. He has said that we could not go there without him, and that he could not accompany us there this week. May one without indiscretion look at this book? You may even take it away if you wish to read it. Since (*ou* as) you have the goodness to lend it to me, I will return it to you to-morrow, or the day after (*sous-entendu* to-morrow). We should like to go a shooting to-morrow, but the weather is not favourable. Ask your sister if she will play us a piece on the piano. What piece do you wish her to play? We will not choose. My brother is calling me, ask him what he wants. He has told me that he wants (*ou* wishes) to speak to you. One spoils children by giving them all they desire (*ou* want). He has told me that he would give me as much (1) as I liked of it (*ou* as many as I liked of them).

THÈME XIX

Sur le verbe FAIRE.

APPLICATION

They make more watches at Geneva than at Paris. One must not do harm to (*ou* hurt) animals. They are making railways everywhere. That will do much good to trade. Do they make beet-root sugar in England? No, the English import their sugar from their colonies. What have you done to-day? I have done all that I promised you to do. The watch-maker is mak-

---

(1) La conjonction *que*, après *autant* et *aussi*, se rend par *as*.

ing me a watch; it will be done (1) for New-year's Day.

When one does not do good for the pleasure of doing it, one generally does it very badly. Do not put off till to-morrow the good action that thou canst do to-day. Not doing good when we can is doing ill (2). Time is badly spent by three sorts of persons: the vicious (*ou* wicked) employ it in doing evil (*ou* ill); the idle, in doing nothing; the vain, in doing too much. What are you doing there? I am

---

(1) *Done*, qui est le participe passé de *do*, s'emploie dans le sens général de fini, achevé; on peut le faire rapporter à l'un ou à l'autre des verbes *to do* ou *to make*.

(2) On pourrait suivre la construction française en disant : *it is doing ill not to do good when we can;* mais l'autre construction est plus conforme au génie de la langue anglaise.

making a cap for my little sister. Have you done your task? I will do it presently.

THEME XX

Sur les Négations.

APPLICATION

Against wearisomeness there is not a more certain remedy than occupation. Politeness is not a science that is learned by rules; it is only an attention to study the tastes of others, and to conform to them. There is no repose so sweet as that which is purchased by labour. Young persons (*ou* people) can never be too attentive to hold their tongues; silence is at once the ornament and the safeguard of youth. There is no expense dearer (*ou* more costly) than that of time: one may sometimes recover one's money; but one can never regain lost time. There is no difficulty that one cannot surmount by constancy (*ou* perseverance). Do not we often see children who have but little talent surpass, by their perseverance, others who, although endowed with good abilities, do not turn them to account, because they do not work with constancy?

Let us not lose our time, for there is not in that respect more difficulty for us than there was for Fénelon, Bossuet, Corneille, and Racine. I have not done all that you gave me to do, I have not had time for it (*ou* to do it). Have you not done your translation?

No, sir, not yet, but I will not forget to do it for to-morrow. I have no dictionary, and I cannot do it without one. There is no ink in the inkstand. Give me some paper, if you please. I have not any. I have no penknife, I cannot mend my pen. Have not you any steel pens? Yes, but they are not good (*ou* good ones) (1).

THÈME XXI

Sur les interrogations.

APPLICATION

My dear children, do you wish to pass a happy life in this world? Are you inclined to make yourselves loved? I assure you that it depends only on

(1) C'est-à-dire quelques-*unes* qui soient bonnes.

yourselves. Have you not a good opportunity of cultivating your minds? Are there more difficulties for you to surmount than there were for such men as Fénelon, Condillac, Fléchier, and other remarkable men who have given lustre to their country? Is it true that you love your parents? prove it by your assiduity. Have they not made, do they not make, will they not make, the greatest sacrifices for you? Do you wish to render them happy? Work to insure your own happiness; is it not what (*ou* that which) they desire?

Do you know that by the exercise of the mind one acquires a fortune which, the more one enjoys it, the more it augments (*ou* the greater it becomes)? What did you know before you commenced (*ou* before commencing) your studies? Had you the least idea of many things which now appear to you very simple and very easy? Are you not very glad to know what you have learned? Well, what you have yet to learn requires only perseverance; with that one may overcome all difficulties.

Has your brother finished his studies? No, not yet. And when shall you finish yours? I shall finish them next year. Were you at the last distribution of prizes? No, I was ill; were there many persons? (*ou* was there much company?) I do not (*ou* don't) (1) know, I was in the country. Shall we go to-morrow to St-Ger-

(1) *Don't*, abrégé de *do not*.

main? Yes, at eight o'clock (1); shall you be ready? Will your brother go? I believe so. Shall we have also the pleasure of seeing your sisters? Shall we return by the railway, or by the stage? Would not the railway be most expeditious? O yes, by far.

---

(1) *O'clock* pour *of the clock,* de la pendule.

DEUXIÈME SECTION

OU

DÉVELOPPEMENT GÉNÉRAL

DES RÈGLES CONTENUES DANS LES THÈMES

DE LA PREMIÈRE SECTION

RECUEIL

De Traits d'Histoire et de Littérature

DÉVELOPPEMENT DES RÈGLES DU THÈME I

Sur l'article indéfini UN, UNE.

One day, I was walking in one of the streets of the city, and I saw a boy with a basket of very fine oranges, which he was offering to every body (*ou* every one) for a shilling a dozen. Thinking it was an opportunity of making a little present to one of my sisters, who is at a school near London, I took a dozen of them, which he gave me in a bag. Having given a shilling to the boy, I was going away; but he called me, saying : Sir! Sir! you have given me a bad piece of money.

I was going to give him another, when a man in a blue uniform came up. He immediately seized the boy by the collar, took him away, telling me to follow him. We soon arrived at a sort of guard-house (station-house), where, on searching the little boy's pockets, he found a number of counterfeit pieces. I need not tell you that the man in blue was a police-officer, nor that the little orange-dealer was a rogue, who only sold his oranges for the purpose of passing his bad money.

He was condemned to a year's imprisonment.

One of the valets de chambre of St-Louis, in sealing a letter, let fall a drop of flaming wax upon one of the legs of that monarch : " You ought to remember," said the king to him, " that my grand-father dismissed you formerly for much less."

One summer's morning, Marshal Turenne, in a little white jacket, with a white cotton nightcap on his head, was leaning over the balcony of a window which looked upon a fine garden. One of the servants, taking him for a cook, gave him a hearty smack behind. Turenne turns round; the servant falls at his feet, and asks his pardon, saying he had taken him for George, one of the scullions. "Well," said the marshal, rubbing himself, "if it had been George, it was not necessary to hit (*ou* you need not have hit) so hard."

DÉVELOPPEMENT DES RÈGLES DU THÈME II

Sur l'article LE, LA, LES.

Absence of Mind

Newton, a native of England, and one of the most celebrated mathematicians that the world has ever produced, was subject to frequent fits of absence of mind, and particularly when he was occupied with the solution of a difficult problem. Then (*ou* on such occasions) he shut himself up in his study, where he sometimes remained the whole day, without even joining the family at table at meal-times. One morning, his house-keeper sent the maid to beg him to come to breakfast; but he answered that he had not the time. Mrs. S. (his house-keeper) then sent the servant back, with an egg and a saucepan. She put the egg upon the table and the saucepan before the fire, telling Mr. Newton that he must let it boil three minutes. Soon afterwards she returned to the study, and found her master before the fire-place with the egg in his hand, and the saucepan on the fire with Mr. Newton's watch, which, through absence of mind, he had put into it instead of the egg.

DÉVELOPPEMENT DES RÈGLES DU THÈME III

Sur le pluriel des Noms.

The Royal Oak

Charles II. (the second), son of the unfortunate Charles I. (the first), king of England, whom the English parliament, under the usurper Cromwell, put to death upon the scaffold, endeavoured several times to conquer (*ou* to recover) by arms the throne of his ancestors; but after having lost (*ou* after losing) many battles, his troops were entirely defeated at Worcester (1).

The adventures of the unhappy

(1) Prononcez *ouerceteur*.

prince after that battle are curious. After having run (*ou* been exposed to) the greatest dangers, he found an asylum and faithful friends at the house of four brothers, husbandmen, of the name of Penderell. There, in order to disguise him, they stained his hands and face, cut his hair, gave him the dress of a wood-cutter (*ou* woodman), and put an axe in his hand. Thus disguised, they led him into the woods.

During some days, the king had for his bed nothing but some straw under the trees. The soldiers of the parliament (*ou* the parliamentary troops) often came there to seek for him, and the king, in order to avoid them, was obliged to climb up an oak, whence (*ou* from which) he saw pass at his feet the people who were seeking him. This venerated oak received, at the restoration, the name of the royal oak, and till about the middle of the eighteenth century, one might see at the fruiterers' (*ou* green-grocers'), in London, on the 29th (twenty-ninth) of May, the anniversary of the preservation of the king, gilded (*ou* gilt) oak-leaves; some persons even wore them in their button-holes on that day.

DÉVELOPPEMENT DES RÈGLES DU THÈME IV

Sur le Genre des Noms

Shipwreck of Prince William

Henry I. (the first), king of England, and son of William the Conqueror, having been detained in France during four years, was preparing to return to England. On his arrival at the port of Harfleur, a sailor (*ou* mariner) named Fitz-Stephen presented himself before him, and offered his vessel for the passage across the straits. The king replied that he had already made choice of a vessel, but that he would willingly confide to him his son, prince William, and the princess Adela with their retinue (*ou* suite), which consisted of the lords and ladies of the court, barons and baronesses, knights and other gentlemen, with their wives. The vessel did not depart until the evening, and by the imprudence of the sailors, excited by the wine which the prince had distributed among them, she (1) struck against a

---

(1) En parlant des navires, les Anglais se ser-

rock, foundered (*ou* sank), and, of three hundred persons, men and women, one only, a butcher of Rouen, named Bérold, was saved.

DÉVELOPPEMENT DES RÈGLES DU THÈME V

Sur le Génitif.

Queen Margaret

During the civil war in England between the houses of York and Lancaster, called the War of the Two Roses, queen Margaret, wife of Henry VI. (the sixth), whom the partisans of the

---

vent toujours des pronoms *she*, elle, au nominatif, et de *her*, la, à l'accusatif, et au possessif pour, son, sa, ses : *She struck*, elle heurta; *I saw her*, je la vis ; *her deck*, son pont; *her cabin*, sa chambre ; *her masts*, ses mâts.

house of York held prisoner in the Tower of London, performed prodigies of valour, in order to maintain the interests of her husband. Continually occupied about the destiny (*ou* the fortunes) of her son, she hastened from one place to another (*ou* from place to place), encouraging the zealous, exciting (*ou* animating) the timid, and exposing herself to the greatest perils. Being alone, one day, with her son in a forest, she was surrounded by a band of robbers, who despoiled (*ou* robbed) her of her gold and jewels. The wretches quarrelled about sharing the jewels, and began a horrible fight.

Margaret, profiting by the confusion, took her son in her arms, and fled into the thickest part of the wood, but after having wandered some time, she was forced to stop, overcome with hunger, fatigue, and fright. The tears of her son augmented her grief, when she perceived that one of the thieves had followed her, sword in hand. Then, with all the energy of despair, advancing towards the brigand, she said to him, "Friend, I confide to thy loyalty the safety of the son of thy king!" The robber, affected (*ou* touched) by that noble confidence, devoted himself to the service of the princess, succeeded in hiding (*ou* concealing) her from the researches of his companions, and conducted her in safety to the quarters of the Lancastrians.

DÉVELOPPEMENT DES RÈGLES DES THÈMES VI ET VII

Sur l'Adjectif.

Clocks

The most ancient means (*ou* methods) employed by civilized people to divide time into equal parts, and which seem to have been the most generally employed, are water-clocks and sun-dials. The first clock with wheels known in France, was sent to Pepin the Short by pope Paul I. (the first), in the year 760 (seven hundred and sixty) of the Christian era. About the year 807 (eight hundred and seven) the caliph Haroun-al-Raschid sent to Charlemagne a very curious clock, but it was not a striking clock, for there were not any till about the fourteenth century. Under Louis XI. (the eleventh), there were portable striking clocks. It is said (*ou* they say) that a gentleman ruined by gaming, being in the king's room, took the prince's clock and hid it in his sleeve, where it happened to strike. Instead of punishing the guilty man, Louis XI. generously gave him what he had stolen.

The first pocket-watches were manufactured at Nuremberg in Germany, in 1500 (one thousand five hundred); they were called Nuremberg eggs, because they were of an oval shape (*ou* form). The invention of repeating watches is due to an Englishman named Barlow, who solicited an exclusive privilege (*ou* a patent) for those kinds of watches; a short time afterwards, a person named Quarre made a superior one, which he presented to James II. (the second), so that the privilege (*ou* patent) was not granted to either of them. A French clock-maker, named Hernais, obtained a patent for pedometer watches; they mark the distance that one goes over, and the number of steps that one makes (*ou* takes).

DÉVELOPPEMENT DES RÈGLES DU THÈME VIII

Sur les Pronoms personnels.

Richard Cœur de Lion

Richard I. (the first), king of England in 1189 (eleven hundred and eighty-nine) was contemporary with

Philip I. (the first) of France; he made with him the second holy war, or crusade against the Saracens, who had driven the Christians from (*ou* out of) Jerusalem. Richard, in consequence of his courage and his daring, was surnamed Lion Heart; but after having escaped all the dangers of war, he met with one of his barons. The viscount (1) of Limoges had discovered upon his estates a treasure, of which he sent to Richard the portion which was due to him as lord paramount (*ou* sovereign lord of the manor); but the king not being satisfied with it, claimed the whole; and as Vidomar, the viscount, refused, he declared war, and marched against him. He

(1) Prononcez *vaïcaounte*.

besieged the castle of Chaluz, which soon offered to capitulate; but Richard replied that he would have all the garrison hanged. He was approaching the walls, when an archer let fly an arrow at him, and wounded him in the left shoulder. He immediately ordered the assault, seized upon the place, and caused all those who had defended it to be hanged, with the exception of the archer who had wounded him. Richard, seeing that he could not recover from the effects of the wound, sent for the archer, and said to him: "What had I done to thee, to drive thee to kill me?" "What had you done to me!" replied he, "you have killed with your own hand my father and my two brothers, and you have sworn to have me hanged (*ou* to hang me); if you have reserved me, it is in order to make me suffer more cruel torments: be it so, I am ready. I shall at least have delivered the world from its greatest scourge." Richard ordered his people to flay him alive, which they were going to do, when the king, feeling the approach of death, ordered them to give a hundred shillings to his murderer, and to set him at liberty; but, instead of obeying, they flayed him, according to the first wish of Richard, and hanged him afterwards upon a gibbet (*ou* and gibbeted him afterwards). Richard died on the 6th (sixth) of April, 1199 (eleven hundred and ninety-nine), at the age of 42 (forty-two) years, having occupied the throne of England from 1189 (eleven hundred and eighty-nine). He was buried (*ou* interred) at Fontevrault in France.

DÉVELOPPEMENT DES RÈGLES DU THÈME IX

Sur les Pronoms ou Adjectifs possessifs.

Brotherly Love

The son of a rich merchant, having abandoned himself in his youth to all kinds of excesses, irritated his father to such a degree that the latter, on his deathbed, made his will and disinherited him, leaving all his wealth to his younger son, who by his good conduct had merited the esteem of all his relations. The elder son, learning the death of his father, and being informed that he had left all his fortune to his brother, reproached himself with (*ou* for) his wildness, saying: "I have well deserved it." This moderation reaches the ears of his brother, who comes (*ou* goes) to see him, embraces him, and addresses him in these words: "Our father, by his will, has bequeathed to me all his wealth; but without doubt (*ou* doubtless) he only wished to deprive of his inheritance the man which you then were, and not him that you now are; it is then with the greatest pleasure that I restore to you the portion which is your due (*ou* which is due to you)."

Leg or Head

Two sailors, at the moment when their vessel was going to fight, had agreed to lend each other mutual assistance in case of need. One of them had his leg carried off by a cannon ball; his shipmate (1) took him upon his shoulders to carry him to the cockpit. On the way, another ball took off the head of the wounded man. His shipmate, not having perceived it, continued his way. — "Where are you going?" said an officer to him. — "I am going to carry my shipmate to our surgeon." — "To the surgeon! why, he has lost his head...." The sailor immediately throws his burden on the deck, exclaiming, "What a liar! upon my soul he told me that he had only lost a leg."

---

(1) *Mate* signifie camarade; *shipmate*, camarade de navire.

DÉVELOPPEMENT DES RÈGLES DU THÈME X

Sur les Pronoms ou Adjectifs relatifs.

A Fox is a Match for a Lion

It is known that almost all the watches that are sold at Paris come from Geneva, and that upon all the line which separates France from Switzerland, smuggling was formerly carried on almost with impunity : there was even, at Geneva, a watch-maker who insured his customers against the import duty, for a trifling sum (*ou* premium). The director-general of the Customs of France, having learnt this, resolved to ascertain by his own experience the reality of the fact. He goes to Geneva, and makes numerous purchases at the watchmaker's of whom we have just spoken, who promises him that he shall receive them duty free. They ask him for his address : " Count ...., director-general of the Customs of France." Very well, sir, you will find those articles at your house on arriving at Paris. — We shall see that, says the Count, who then goes to his inn, orders post-horses and sets off. On arriving at the frontier, he gives to the officers of the Customs the description of the little case (*ou* casket) which contained the jewels, and promises a hundred louis to him who shall seize it. He continues his journey with all the celerity that can be obtained of postilions, who, in the hope of gaining a few sous more, exhaust the strength of the unfortunate animals that are confided to them.

At last the Count arrives in Paris, and alights at the hotel which serves as a residence for the directors of the Customs. He embraces his family, and then goes towards his study (*ou* closet) : what does he behold?... the case of watches placed upon the chimney-piece (*ou* mantel-piece) as if on purpose to defy (*ou* to mock) him. The cunning watchmaker had bribed one of the director's servants, and the latter had slipped the case into the carriage, which the officers had respected. It was therefore Count...., director of the Customs of France, who was the smuggler.

DÉVELOPPEMENT DES RÈGLES DU THÈME XI

Sur les Pronoms démonstratifs.

Better and Better

Joseph II. (the second), emperor of Germany, used often to take a ride alone in a calash which he drove himself, in the environs (*ou* neighbourhood) of Vienna. One morning, when riding in that manner, he was caught in (*ou* overtaken by) the rain. He was yet at some distance, when a sergeant begged him to give him a place in his carriage : " It would not inconvenience you much, said the latter, and would save my uniform, which I have put on to-day for the first time. — Let us save your uniform, my brave fellow, says the emperor, and place yourself (*ou* sit down) there. Whence do you come? — Why, faith, I come from the house of a guard (*ou* game-keeper), one of my friends (*ou* a friend of mine), where I have made a famous breakfast. — What have you then eaten so very good? — Guess. — How should I know? Some egg-flip? — O yes, egg-flip indeed! better than that. — Sour crout? — Better than that. — A loin of veal? — Better still. — Oh, by my faith, in this manner I shall never guess, says Joseph. — A pheasant, my brave fellow, a pheasant caught in the preserves of his majesty (*ou* in his majesty's preserves), replies the sergeant, slapping him on the thigh. — Ah! caught in his majesty's preserves, it must have been all the better for that. — I answer for it (*ou* I believe you)."

As they were approaching the town, Joseph asked his companion where he lodged, in order that he might set him down at home (*ou* at his own house). The sergeant, thanking him, begged to know who was the person from whom he received (*ou* to whom he was indebted for) that politeness. "Now it is your turn, said the prince; guess. — You are a soldier, sir? — As you say, sir. — A lieutenant? — O yes, lieutenant (1) indeed! better than that. — Captain? — Better than that. — Colonel perhaps? — Better than that, I tell you. — What the devil! says the other, can you be a field marshal? —

---

(1) Prononcez *leftenante.*

Better than that (*ou* better still). —Ah, my god! it's (1) the emperor.—Himself, says Joseph, unbuttoning his coat to show his decorations : his Majesty who has regaled (*ou* treated) you with that fine pheasant." The sergeant, confounded, supplicates the emperor to let him alight. "No no, no no; after having eaten my pheasant, you shall be able to boast that I have conducted you home."

DÉVELOPPEMENT DES RÈGLES DU THÈME XII

Sur ON.

An Adventure of Scarron

It is known, or, if it is not known, it ought to be known, that Scarron,

---

(1) *It's*, abrégé de *it is*.

the celebrated satirical author, husband of Madame de Maintenon, had become a cripple. This is what they relate on that subject in his country, Le Mans. One Shrove Tuesday, everybody was assembled, on foot, on horseback, and in carriages, grotesquely dressed, each in his own way, and they were following the road to Angers; they endeavoured to attract attention by committing all sorts of follies. Scarron, being at Le Mans during the carnival, wished to distinguish himself above all the others. You would never guess what he did: he rubs himself all over the body with honey, and crack! he throws himself into a cask (*ou* tub) full of feathers. Scarcely has he appeared in the street, when the people, astonished at seeing such a monster, assemble tumultuously around him, and pursue him. They forget everything else to run after this bird of a new species; boys collect from all parts, and stones fly at the head of the monster. Scarron takes to his heels, and can scarcely escape from the populace. Exhausted with fatigue, and dripping with perspiration, he arrives at Pontlieu, throws himself into the river Huisne, and, finding that they had lost sight of him, he crouches under an arch of the bridge, where he remains half a day, without daring to move from the place. On the arrival of night, he succeeds in escaping. But poor Scarron, from that time, remained all his life a cripple.

DÉVELOPPEMENT DES RÈGLES DU THÈME XIII

Sur EN.

Origin of New-year's Gifts (1)

Many children, and even grown persons, occupy themselves about étrennes (new-year's gifts), and often talk of them without knowing the signification of the term. You will not perhaps be sorry to find here a few words relating to that subject, and which will give an idea of it. The word *étrennes* comes from the Latin ***strenæ,*** and in the ancient authors we find it with an *s*, ***estrennes***.— It is said that Tatius, king of Rome in

(1) *New-year's gifts*, cadeaux de la nouvelle année.

the eighth century before Jesus Christ, having received as happy presage (*ou* good omen) some branches cut in a wood consecrated to the goddess *Strenua*, that is to say, the goddess of strength, and which were presented to him on the first day of the year (*ou* New-year's Day), authorised that custom, and gave the name of *strenæ* to those presents, in memory of that goddess, who presided at the ceremony of étrennes.

Bellingen also, in his Etymologies, speaks of it in the following manner: —" The day of the calends of January was celebrated at Rome in honour of Janus. Relations and friends sent to each other reciprocally, on that day, presents which they called *strenæ*. The custom had been introduced by king Tatius, a companion of Romulus, founder of Rome, when he went the first to gather in the sacred wood of the goddess Strenua the fortunate branches which were the presages of the new year. They (the Romans), on meeting, added to their salutations, wishes for happiness, and desires for prosperity for the whole year. Such is the origin of étrennes (new-year's gifts), and of the felicitations which we address to each other at the beginning of every year."

DÉVELOPPEMENT DES RÈGLES DU THÈME XIV

Sur Y.

Thoughtlessness and Mischief

M. de Martainville, a young counsellor at the parliament of Normandy, had assembled at his country-seat near Montivilliers a score of young madcaps to pass the vacation there. They played all sorts of tricks; they pierced (*ou* bored) the walls and the ceilings in order to pass cords through them, which cords they had fastened to your curtains, and your blankets; they dug holes concealed under the grass, to make people fall into them; they put salt into your coffee, pepper into your snuff, chopped horsehair, crabs (*ou* crayfish), and frogs into your bed, so that one could not go and pay a visit to this country-seat without being exposed to all sorts of pranks that one might even call impertinences.

M. de Martainville and his wife expected at their house the widow of the intendant of Alençon, Madame Hérault de Séchelles, whom they had invited to come and repose herself during some days at Martainville. It is proper to tell you that she was an old woman excessively susceptible, that she was recovering from a serious indisposition (*ou* illness); that she had an income of 60,000 (sixty thousand) livres, and that the Martainvilles were her principal heirs.

Mind! said M. de Martainville to this troop of young counsellors, don't go and play any tricks during the stay of my aunt de Séchelles; be prudent, gentlemen, and do not forget that she is very rich, and that we hope to inherit her fortune. — The master of the house had never seen this aunt of his wife, and the latter had not seen her since the age of five or six years; a fine opportunity for playing some new trick! It was in fact so fine, and the temptation so great that, in spite of the advice of M. de Martainville, the young fellows could not resist it. — One of them therefore thought proper to disguise himself as an old woman, and to arrive post at the mansion, accompanied by another, disguised as a chambermaid; but the plot was divulged. They got up (*ou* organized) a counter-plot, and prepared to hoax the hoaxers (*ou* to trick the tricksters).

While they were on the watch in order to receive them handsomely (*ou* to give them a warm reception) the real aunt arrived. Thinking it was the impostor, they fell upon her, tore off her flounced dress, her collar, her wig, in fact they so cruelly ill-treated her that she fell under the blows, and remained lying upon the pavement of the hall, and they perceived at length that it was the real aunt. They then gave her all possible assistance, but she died three days after.

M. de Martainville, from delicacy, in order to silence (*ou* prevent) injurious suspicions, did not claim any part of Madame de Séchelles' property. He abandoned it to his relations.

DÉVELOPPEMENT DES RÈGLES DU THÈME XV

Sur Y AVOIR.

Voyage round the world

The celebrated navigator Bougainville was passing in a post-chaise through the Champs-Elysées; there was a great number of people, and among the crowd, M. B. perceives one of his friends who was walking there. Immediately he orders the postilion to stop, and alights from the carriage. Good morning, my friend, says he, it is an age since I have seen thee; I am going to Versailles, come there and dine with me. — Impossible, I am engaged. — Nonsense, thou wilt not refuse me, there will be a dinner to thy taste (*ou* liking).

Half persuaded, and half forced, M.*** gets into the carriage... They arrive at Versailles, the carriage passes through the town without stopping: then said the friend: But there is no appearance that we shall dine at Versailles, as we have already passed it.—It is no longer possible to conceal the truth from thee, replied M. B., we are going to dine at one of my kinsmen's a few leagues farther. The other began to be angry, but it was useless. — At length the carriage stops, they alight, enter at an innkeeper's, and dine.

"Now that I see thee a little calmed (*ou* appeased) I will tell thee the truth; I am going to Havre, it is only twenty (*ou* a score of) leagues farther, and thou wilt not leave me: thou hast not any linen or clothes (1), it is true; but there is in my trunk enough for two."

"Be it so, said the other, I consent." The two travellers start (*ou* set off) again; they arrive at Havre. Bougainville then says to M.***: "Thou wilt come with me and see my ship, which is yonder in the roadstead, wilt thou not?"

"With all my heart," says the other, and they are both soon on board. "My friend, said M. B., they were only waiting for me to weigh anchor; I am going to make a voyage round the world, come with me, thou shalt want for nothing..." And, without waiting an answer, he gives the signal for sailing. M.***, seeing that it was im-

---

(1) Prononcez *cloze*.

possible to retract, accepted this singular proposal, and thus unexpectedly made his voyage round the world.

DÉVELOPPEMENT DES RÈGLES DU THÈME XVI

Sur IL FAUT.

National Fashions

The following anecdote is found in a dictionary of morals and literature by Capelle.—A king of Salee, a town in Africa, having learned that there was among his slaves a celebrated painter, sent for him and said to him : You must paint me a picture for my gallery.—Willingly, sire, replies the artist, hoping perhaps by that means to regain (*ou* to purchase) his liberty;

how must I do it? — You must represent in it a person of every nation that you know; they must also be represented so naturally that one may be able to distinguish each of them by his air and his dress.—I will do it in my best manner (*ou* as well as I can) replies the slave, but your majesty must procure me the materials.—You shall have all that you want, said the king; but the picture must be finished for the festival of Ramazan.

All being ready, the painter set to work; he dressed every one in the fashion of his country, except the Frenchman, whom he left naked, bearing on his bended arm a piece of cloth. The picture being completed, the monarch was informed of it. He came to see it, but as soon as he perceived it, he went into a passion with the painter, saying : You must have been mad (*ou* out of your mind) to paint the Frenchman without clothes.—My lord, replied the artist, be not surprised at it, I thought it was necessary to leave him so, because he changes his fashion so often, that my art, not knowing on which to fix, has given him cloth in order that he may suit himself at his pleasure. — *Ou en vers :*

> So often he changes his style,
> That my art, quite unable to guess,
> I have given him cloth the mean while
> To make, as he fancies, his dress.

DÉVELOPPEMENT DES RÈGLES DU THÈME XVII

Sur DEVOIR.

Desperate Valour.

Captain Casa-Bianca, a native of Corsica, commanded the Orient, the vessel of Admiral Brueix, who was to conduct Napoleon and his army in the expedition to Egypt. The young Casa-Bianca, son of the captain, was serving on board the same vessel as a marine guard, when, on the 1st (first) of August, 1798 (seventeen hundred and ninety-eight), an English fleet, commanded by Admiral Nelson, attacked the French vessels before (*ou* off) Aboukir, near the mouth of the Nile. The sailors of the two bravest nations in the world fought most desperately.

It was necessary (*ou* they were) to conquer or die; it is the duty of brave men who fight against the enemies of their country, and never was duty better fulfilled (*ou* performed). At length a cannon ball cut the brave admiral in two; Captain Casa-Bianca received at the same instant a mortal wound, and the vessel had already taken fire. They came to inform (*ou* to warn) young Casa-Bianca that he ought to provide for his own safety, for the fire had already penetrated into all parts of the vessel.

The brave youth replied: "I have not forgotten what one owes to one's country, ought I to forget what one owes to one's father?" Saying this, he embraces him closely, and swears that he will not quit him. Then the commodore of the squadron ties himself to the stump of a mast thrown into the sea. Young Casa-Bianca ties his dying father to it also, and places himself on it. The three unfortunates, floating at the mercy of the waves, would perhaps have been saved : but being too near the burning vessel, they were swallowed up in the billows at the moment when, the fire reaching the powder magazine, the vessel blew up with a frightful crash.

DÉVELOPPEMENT DES RÈGLES DU THÈME XVIII

Sur POUVOIR et VOULOIR.

Filial affection.

In 1720 (seventeen hundred and twenty), the czar (1) Peter, wishing to abolish the custom of wearing beards, forbade it by proclamation. The people declared that they would not obey, and that nobody could force them to cut off their beards. An insurrection followed, but it was soon put down, and eight thousand people, it is said, were massacred. The czar chose a vast plain near Moscow. They surrounded this place with pa-

(1) Prononcer *zar*.

lisades through (*ou* between) which one could see; and after having placed several blocks there, they brought the unfortunates who were to lose their lives. Peter himself, desirous of giving (*ou* setting) the example to the executioner (*ou* headsman), took an axe in his hand; many courtiers imitated him, and Menzikoff, the favourite, boasted of having cut off the most (*ou* the greatest number of) heads.

In the midst of this scene of carnage, a child of about twelve years of age came and placed his head upon the block of the czar (*ou* the czar's block), but the latter, not wishing to strike, took him by the arm and pushed him away. The boy, without saying a single word, went and placed himself upon another block. The czar, who perceived it, advanced towards him, raised him, and put him away again. A moment after, the boy came to place himself again under the axe.

Peter, unable to contain himself any longer, asked him angrily why he wished that they should cut off his head : "You have cut off that of my father, that of my brother, and those of all my relations, who were not more guilty than I am", said the boy to him; "why will you not cut off mine? I cannot and will not survive them." The czar did not reply, but he caused the boy to be driven away from the enclosure, threw down his axe, and went away.

DÉVELOPPEMENT DES RÈGLES DU THÈME XIX

Sur le verbe FAIRE.

Mary Stuart.

The following anecdote makes a part of the history of the extraordinary events which marked the life of Mary Stuart. This Scottish princess, at the age of sixteen years, married Francis II. (the second) of France, who left her a widow at the end of two years and a half. Her mother, the regent of Scotland, being dead, Mary returned to her own country, and took the government of it; but very soon, a victim to the troubles which disturbed the kingdom, she was confined in the castle of Loch-

Leven, under the care of the Earl of Douglas.

The son of that lord, seeing that the captive queen did nothing but weep and sob, was so much afflicted by it that one day he went to her apartment and said to her : "Madam, the tears that I see you shed cause me so much pain, that I would procure you an opportunity of quitting this sad dwelling, and if you will believe me I have the means of doing it. At the base of this tower they have made a door, by which we go out to make excursions on the lake ; I will bring you the key of it ; I will have the boat ready, and I will flee with you, because my father would never pardon (*ou* forgive) me for what I am going to do."

The queen accepts the offer; she writes with charcoal upon her handkerchief, for want of pen and paper, and finds means to impart her design to some friends who had remained faithful to her. The boy having delivered the key to the queen, she went out of the castle, accompanied by her deliverer; they gained (*ou* reached) the other shore of the lake, and there found their partisans.

But Mary did not long enjoy her liberty; her troops having been defeated by the rebels, she took refuge in England, where Queen Elizabeth put her to death, after twenty years' imprisonment, under the accusation of having conspired against her life and her throne.

DÉVELOPPEMENT DES RÈGLES DU THÈME XX

Sur les Négations.

Charlemagne.

Young people cannot read too much (*ou* too often) the history of the reign of Charlemagne. Until his time, there were in France none but the clergy who occupied themselves with the study of literature. But that great monarch was not satisfied with his glory as a warrior : he wished for nothing less than a victory over the human mind. He visited the schools, encouraging the scholars.—"Study", exclaimed he, "do not lose the opportunity of instructing yourselves, of preparing for yourselves happiness ;

apply yourselves. I will not forget, I will not fail to reward you and to show my esteem for you."

He presided at the examinations. Being one day dissatisfied at the little progress of some young students whom he assembled in the school of his palace, he said to them :

"Because you are rich, and are sons of the first families in my kingdom, you believe that your birth and your riches will be sufficient for you, that you have no need of those studies which would do you so much honour ; you take pleasure in a voluptuous and effeminate life ; you think only of dress, of gaming, and of pleasures ; but I swear to you that I attach no importance to your nobility or to your riches ; and if you do not recover as soon as possible, by assiduous study, the time that you have lost in frivolities, you must not hope for encouragement or protection from me; never, no never, shall you obtain anything from Charles. Do not forget this warning."

DÉVELOPPEMENT DES RÈGLES DU THÈME XXI

Sur les INTERROGATIONS.

The Female Hussar.

About the end of the year 1806 (eighteen hundred and six), Napoleon was holding a grand review of troops in the Champ de Mars. When he arrived at the sixth hussars, he perceived a soldier who was prancing about out of the ranks. He cried out immediately : "Why is not that hussar at his post? let him be put under arrest for eight days." — "Sire", replied the colonel, "permit me to solicit pardon for my volunteer; you will not refuse it to me when you have interrogated him." — "Well!" said the emperor, "let him come."

The hussar approaches, and Napoleon says to him : "Your name?" — "My emperor, they call me Breton-Double." — "Why have you left the ranks?" — "I have never entered them; I have always followed the regiment as a volunteer." — "How long have you been attached to the regiment?" — "These eight years." — "What induced you to enter the service?" — "My love for my country and for my husband." — "What? you are a woman?" — "Yes, sire, and you will never have an arm more devoted than mine." "Who is your husband?" — "Poncet, a quarter-master." — "Have you any children?" — "Yes, sire, one boy." — "What does he do?" (*ou* what is he?) — "He is a trumpeter in the eleventh dragoons." — "Do you know the exercise?" — "Yes, sire, and the broadsword also." — "We shall see that, said Napoleon." "Colonel, call out a platoon; Breton-Double, enter the ranks." The colonel ordered the evolutions, and the emperor with astonishment beheld a woman manage a horse with the vigour and confidence of a soldier of ten campaigns. "Breton-Double", said Napoleon, " there is something for your stripes; go and rejoin your regiment; we shall see each other again."

The sixth hussars went off for the campaign of Prussia, and at the battle of Eylau Breton-Double distinguished herself so much that the emperor rewarded her with a gold medal. At the battle of Friedland, also, this woman, although badly wounded in the thigh and in the armpit, behaved so heroically, and did so much harm to the enemy, that Napoleon, affected by so much devotedness and bravery, took off his cross of honour, and placed it upon her breast. At length, at the battle of Waterloo, Breton-Double paid her last tribute to France, which she had served during seventeen years.

She had her leg broken there, and Poncet, her husband, who had become captain, died by her side. Amputated on the field of battle, she was taken up by the enemy, who took her to England, where she passed six years, honoured and welcomed wherever she went. At the death of Louis XVIII. (the eighteenth) she returned to France, and obtained from Charles X. (the tenth) a pension of 280 (two hundred and eighty) francs.

Since the revolution of 1830 (eighteen hundred and thirty) they say that she has received the arrears of her cross (*ou* decoration), a pension as a captain's widow, and her half pay as a disabled quarter-master. Her son, who had become a captain in the eleventh dragoons, followed his master to the island of Elba.

Nota. Au mois d'août 1851 cette femme vivait encore. Je l'ai rencontrée au jardin du palais de Versailles. La croix que lui donna Napoléon brillait encore sur sa poitrine. PERCY SADLER.

TROISIÈME SECTION

ANECDOTES HISTORIQUES

Gratitude and Ingratitude.

The following anecdote is found in the ancient chronicles of Britain, now England. King Lear, who reigned 800 (eight hundred) years before the birth of Jesus-Christ, had three daughters, named Goneril, Regan, and Cordelia. At an advanced age, he conceived the project of sharing (*ou* dividing) his states among his children, in proportion to the filial affection they bore (*ou* felt for) him. He interrogated them separately. — Goneril and Regan replied that they loved him, and would love him constantly, better than any person or anything in the world. Cordelia, the youngest, more natural and more true, told him that she loved him tenderly, and as one ought to love one's father.

Lear, dissatisfied with that answer, which he thought cold, in comparison with the protestations of the two elder, gave the southern province to Goneril, whom he married to the duke of Cornwall, and the provinces of the north to Regan, whose hand was granted to the duke of Albany; and he reserved for himself the middle (*ou* midland) provinces of the kingdom.

Cordelia, although disinherited, married a king of Neustria, who loved her for her virtues and her beauty.

The ambitious duchesses, wishing to get rid of their father, soon made war against him, and Lear, dethroned by his own daughters, found no asylum but with Cordelia. She assembles a considerable army, takes the command of it, crosses the straits, defeats the rebels, restores the throne to her father, reunites at his death the whole inheritance, and reigns during five years adored by her subjects.

Meanwhile, the sons of Goneril and Regan, ashamed of obeying a woman, only waited an opportunity of revenging their mothers. They formed a conspiracy, assembled some warriors, and in the tumult succeeded in obtaining possession of the person of their aunt. Thrown into (*ou* exposed to) the horrors of a dungeon, threatened with the greatest outrages, the unfortunate daughter of Lear took away her own life, in order to avoid the torments they were preparing for her. But they two cousins, jealous of each other, disputed the crown; a sanguinary battle took place, in which Cymedage succumbed (*ou* was defeated), and the other, named Morgan, ascended the throne.

Malebranche's Leg of Mutton.

We find in history, both ancient and modern, many examples of freaks of imagination, from which some great men have not been exempt. Malebranche, a celebrated philosopher of the seventeenth century, was, it is said, during a long time the sport (*ou* victim) of a singular idea. He imagined that he had continually an enormous leg of mutton at the end of his nose. One accosted him: "How is M. Malebranche?" (*ou* how does M. Malebranche do?) — "Very well in other respects, but this horrible leg of mutton becomes insupportable to me by its weight and its smell."—"How, this leg of mutton?" —"Yes, don't you see it there, hanging?" —If one laughed, or if one denied it, Malebranche became seriously angry. One of his friends, a witty man, wishing to cure him, thought it would be well, on paying him a visit, to notice his embarrassment, and to ask him about it.

The good father embraces with expressions of gratitude this first believer, who, drawing back, uttered a cry.— " I have hurt you, my friend?" "Certainly you have, your leg of mutton has hurt my eye. But I cannot comprehend how it is that you have not sought before now (*ou* sooner) to get rid of that inconvenience. If you will permit me, with a razor it is an operation without any sort of danger."—" My friend! my friend! I shall owe you more than my life... Oh! oh dear! oh!" In the twinkling of an eye, the friend had slightly grazed the end of the nose, and taking from under his cloak a superb leg of mutton, held it up in triumph. " Ah!" exclaimed Malebranche, " I live, I breathe, I am saved, my nose is free... but... it was raw... and this is cooked."—"I should think it is, during the hour that you have been before the fire."

From that time Malebranche suffered no more persecution from his leg of mutton... and he became Malebranche.

One can do good at every age.

As soon as young Napoleon (1) could speak, he became, like nearly all children, a great inquirer. He was very fond of seeing the people who walked in the garden and in the courtyard of the Tuileries. Having remarked that many persons entered the palace with great rolls of paper,

(1) Fils de Napoléon Ier.

he asked his governess, Madame de Montesquiou, what it signified (*ou* what was the meaning of it). The latter told him that they were unfortunate people who came to ask some favour of his father. From that time (*ou* moment), every time that he saw a petition, he cried, wept, and had no peace until they had brought it (*ou* until it was brought) to him, and he never failed to present to his father, every day at his breakfast, those which he had thus collected on the previous day. One may easily judge that when this custom became known to the public (*ou* became publicly known), they did not let the child want petitions.

He saw, one day, under his windows, a woman in mourning, holding by the hand a little boy three or four years old, also in mourning. The latter held in his hand a petition which he showed, at a distance, to the young prince. The child wished to know why that poor little fellow was dressed all in black. The governess answered him that it was doubtless because his father was dead. He expressed to her a great desire to speak to this child. Madame de Montesquiou, who seized all opportunities of increasing his sensibility, consented to it, and gave orders that he should be introduced, with his mother. She was a widow, whose husband had been killed in the last campaign, and who, finding herself without resource, solicited a pension.

Young Napoleon took the petition,

and promised to deliver it to his papa. The next day he made up his customary packet (*ou* parcel), but he kept separately the petition in which he took a particular interest; and after having delivered to the emperor the other petitions all together : "Papa", said he, "here is a petition from a little boy who is very unhappy. His father died for thee; give him a pension." Napoleon took his son in his arms, embraced him tenderly, granted the pension, and had the warrant made out for it in the course of the day.

Curiosity and Indiscretion.

There are two sorts of curiosity : one of interest, which prompts us to learn what may be useful to us; the other of indiscretion, the fault of children who know nothing, and of fools who meddle with the follies of others.

We seldom (*ou* rarely) find these two kinds of curiosity in the same person; history, however, furnishes some examples of it, and among others that of M. de la Condamine, whose scientific researches have been so useful to geography.

One day when he was paying a visit to Madame de ***, he found her sitting at her secretary, and writing a letter to one of her friends. She asked him permission to continue, in order not to miss the post. M. de la Condamine answered in the politest (*ou* most polite) manner in the world: "Most certainly, madam."

Induced, however, by his insurmountable curiosity, he placed himself behind the lady's chair, whence he read every phrase as it dropped (*ou* flowed) from her pen. A looking-glass inside the secretary soon revealed to her this indiscretion, and she conceived the ingenious idea of continuing in these terms: "I would say much more to you, my dear friend, if M. de la Condamine were not reading behind me." Scarcely had she traced those words, when our inquisitivê gentleman, quite bewildered, cries out: "I beg your pardon, madam, I assure you that I was not reading."

Misfortunes which happened to Charles VI., King of France.

In the year 1393 (thirteen hundred and ninety-three) Charles VI. (the sixth) wishing to revenge himself on Montfort, Duke of Brittany, who had sent some persons to assassinate Clisson the constable, assembled an army at Mans, and put himself at the head of it. In crossing the forest of Mans, the king had but a small retinue, because they did not wish him to be inconvenienced by the dust. Suddenly a man in his shirt, bare-headed and bare-footed, rushed from between two trees, seized the bridle of the king's horse, and cried out to him in a hoarse voice: "King, ride no farther; return, thou art betrayed." He held the reins so fast that they were obliged to strike him to make him let go; but they did not arrest him, and he disappeared. The king did not say a word, but they remarked a change in his countenance, and a sort of trembling agitate his body.

On going out of the forest, they entered on a sandy plain, which, being heated by a burning sun, reflected an insupportable heat. The king was accompanied by two pages only; one of them, almost asleep, let his lance fall upon the helmet of the other. Charles, aroused by that noise from the reverie in which he was plunged, thinks it is the accomplishment of the warning that the mysterious man had just given him; he draws his sword, spurs on his horse, strikes all those whom he finds in his way, crying out: "Forward! forward upon the traitors!" It is said that he killed four men in that attack (*ou* fit) of frenzy. At length his sword breaks, and his strength becomes exhausted. Then one of his chamberlains leaps upon the crupper of his horse and seizes him. They disarm him, place him senseless in a waggon, and take him back to Mans, where he remained during six months in a state of complete madness.

The Masked Ball.

The health of king Charles VI. (the sixth) having become pretty good, the queen, on the occasion of the marriage of a young lady of her court, gave a grand festival, followed by a masked ball. The king came to it, disguised as a savage (*ou* wild man) conducting five young lords disguised like himself, and fastened together by an iron chain. Their dresses were made of linen covered with pitch, on which they had applied tow (*ou* flax). The duke of Orleans, curious to know who the maskers were, approaches one of them with a flambeau; a spark falls, the tow takes fire, and the flames soon envelope them all.

Amidst the screams (*ou* howlings) of these unfortunates, who were in vain endeavouring to break their chain, a piercing cry is distinguished: " Save the king! Save the king! " The cry proceeded from the queen, who fainted. The Duchess of Berry, near whom the king happened to be, covered him with her cloak, and thus smothered the flames. Of the five wild slaves, four died in dreadful torments. One alone broke the chain, ran to the butlery, threw himself into a tub full of water, and was saved. The king was not much hurt, but it is believed that this accident made a strong impression upon him, for he soon after had a relapse of his disorder.

It is remarkable enough that royal

marriages in France have often been attended (*ou* accompanied) by serious accidents. At the rejoicings given on the occasion of the marriage of Louis XVI. (the sixteenth), then dauphin, more than twelve hundred persons perished in the Champs-Élysées. At the marriage of Napoleon with Marie-Louise, from twenty to thirty distinguished personages were victims of the fire at the hotel of Prince Schwartzenberg, in the rue de Provence; and at the marriage of the duke of Orleans, in 1837 (eighteen hundred and thirty-seven), the Champ de Mars was witness of a tragic event, which cost the lives of a score of persons, who were trampled under foot and crushed to death.

Sad Mistake.

The unfortunate accident (1) which happened on the 30th (thirtieth) of May, 1770 (seventeen hundred and seventy), at the close of the festival given by the city of Paris on the marriage of the dauphin, will not be forgotten for a long time. The authorities had imprudently neglected to clear (*ou* disencumber) the issues from the place Louis XV (the fifteenth), where the fireworks were let off, and the pickpockets did not fail to go there, to increase the disorder and profit by it. A horrible butchery (*ou* massacre)

(1) On pourrait, au lieu de prendre la tournure passive, tourner par l'active en commençant par *We shall not forget for a long time*, etc.

was the result of all these deplorable circumstances; more than a thousand persons were trodden under foot, crushed to death or precipitated into the ditches that surrounded the place.

In this crowd was a young man, having under his protection a young lady whom he was (1) to marry on the following day. Protecting his betrothed, walking before her to make way for her, the young man supported her steps and her courage for a long time amidst the cries uttered by the victims who were falling at every moment. At length, he hears the voice of his betrothed. " I am fainting ", said she, " my strength fails me, I can-

---

(1) Voyez ma Grammaire pratique, p. 269, pour le cas où le verbe *devoir* se rend par *to be*, etc.

not go any farther."—"There is yet a resource", cried the young man, almost in despair: "get upon my shoulders." Immediately he feels that his advice has been followed, and the desire of saving her that he loved doubles his strength. He resists the most violent shocks, he struggles, and at length gets clear of the crowd.

Having arrived at (*ou* reached) one of the extremities of the place, after having deposited upon a bench his precious burden, palpitating, exhausted, dying with fatigue, but intoxicated with joy, he turns... it was not she!... Another, more nimble, had profited by the advice; his beloved was no more!

The Fire of London.

In the night between the 2nd (second) and 3rd (third) of September, 1666 (sixteen hundred and sixty-six), a fire broke out in the heart (*ou* middle) of that part of London called the City, a very populous and very commercial quarter. The neighbouring houses, full of combustible goods, soon became a prey to the flames. The fire-engines being out of order, the water failed, and the wind, which was blowing with extreme violence, carried the fire from roof to roof with the rapidity of lightning. The whole town soon presented the spectacle of an immense column of flames of more than a mile in diameter, which, in rising, curling, and dividing itself, filled the air with innumerable particles of fire, everywhere spreading new conflagrations.

This horrible destruction extended itself in all directions during two nights and two days; at length, on the 5th (fifth) of September, the king (Charles the Second) and his brother, the Duke of York, who had gone wherever the danger was greatest, contrived, by destroying rows of buildings, to save the Temple Church, Westminster Abbey, and the palace of Whitehall. On Thursday, the 6th (sixth), the wind moderated, and they hoped to master the fire; but in the evening it again broke out furiously in the environs of the Tower. They blew up houses with gunpowder; in this manner they made large openings, and succeeded in confining the fire to the quarters already consumed. Thirteen thousand two hundred houses, and eighty-nine churches were reduced to ashes. Two hundred thousand individuals, in the most absolute destitution, slept on the ground in the neighbourhood of London. The king, the princes, the ministers of state, and the population of the rest of the kingdom came to their assistance, and they distributed them in the neighbouring towns and villages, where they found all the hospitality that charity and sympathy can inspire.

Honours Rendered (*ou* paid) to Animals.

Ancient history furnishes us with numerous examples of honours rendered (*ou* paid) to animals. Alexander the Great, King of Macedon, had a horse named Bucephalus, which, it is said, would not suffer himself to be mounted except by his master, for whom he always knelt down (*ou* went on his knees). At a battle in Asia, Bucephalus received a mortal wound: he set off immediately, carried his rider out of danger, which he had scarcely done when he fell dead. That horse was then thirty years old (*ou* of age). Alexander loved him so much that in memory of him he built a town to which he gave the name of Bucephalus.

Caligula, a Roman emperor, as celebrated by his follies as by his cruelties, had a horse named Incitatus, to which he rendered the most extraordinary honours. He appointed him pontiff, and made him a consul; he had (1) made for him a stable in marble (*ou* a marble stable), an ivory manger, a blanket (*ou* cloth) of purple, and a collar of pearls. This horse ate at his table; the emperor himself helped him to (*ou* fed him with) gilded barley, and offered him wine in a golden cup, out of which he him-

(1) Lorsque le verbe *faire* est suivi d'un autre verbe à l'infinitif, celui-là se rend par le verbe *avoir*, et l'infinitif se met au participe passé. Voyez Grammaire pratique, p. 118.

self had first drunk. It is said that the senators, feeling but little flattered at having such a colleague, hastened his death.

These examples of honours rendered to animals in ancient times ought not to astonish us more than what is practised even now, in different parts of the Indies.

The Indians, who believe in metempsychosis, are persuaded that a body so majestic as that of the elephant can only be animated by the soul of a great man, or a king. At Siam, at Laos, at Pegu, they respect, even to veneration, the white elephants, as enclosing the living manes of the emperors of India. They have each a palace, a household consisting of a numerous retinue, a service of gold plate, choice meats (*ou* food), and magnificent clothes (1). They pay homage to them, offering them the richest and rarest objects.

As a proof that this superstition exists at present in all its force, we offer the following extract from the *Asiatic Journal* of the 30th (thirtieth) of May, 1837 (eighteen hundred and thirty-seven):

" A letter from Siam announces to us that in consequence of the indisposition of the white elephant of the king of that country, all business is at a stand: the king does not give audience to anybody; all the princes and ministers of state, as well as the

---

(1) Prononcez *clôze*.

other officers, are obliged to attend, night and day, upon the illustrious patient; they are even forced to take their meals in presence of the elephant. The king himself pays him twice a day his tribute of respect, presenting him his food with his royal hand, begging him not to abandon him, but to stay and govern the country with him. They even say that his Siamese Majesty shed tears on the occasion. The elephant is also continually surrounded by priests, who recite prayers for his recovery."

A Fine (*ou* noble) Trait in the Character of Charles V.

The following circumstance is cited as having happened in his youth: one day, pursuing a wild boar with more ardour than prudence, he found himself in the midst of a forest, followed only by the Count de Bossu. The prince perceives that the young lord has wounded himself with his hunting-knife, which, according to the custom of that time, was poisoned with the juice of henbane. The only means of arresting the progress of that poison is to suck the wound immediately. The prince does not hesitate an instant, and in spite of the danger, and the resistance of the young count, he procures him the necessary assistance. The prince had also distinguished himself by his assiduity and his constancy in his studies. His success in the living languages had been such that he sometimes said he would employ Italian to converse with the pope, Spanish to speak to the queen Jane, his mother, English to speak to queen Catherine, his aunt, Flemish to speak to his friends, and French to speak with himself.

The Earl, the King, and the Painter.

Holbein, the celebrated painter, being at the court of Henry VIII. (the eighth) of England, that prince employed him to paint a picture, and forbade him at the same time to show it to any one. An earl, curious to see him handle the brush, came and knocked at his door. The painter answers him that he is not permitted to open it ; the lord persists, and the painter begins to grow angry. At length, not being able to get rid of the importunate personage, he runs to the door, opens it, and seizing the earl, throws him from top to bottom of the stairs. Holbein then ran to the king, and related the adventure to him ; Henry forgave him, on condition of his asking pardon of the earl.

The earl arrives soon after, seriously wounded, and his face covered with blood ; he demands justice. The king pities (1) him, and exhorts him to pardon ; but finding him inflexible, and foreseeing that sooner or later he would play Holbein a foul trick, he exclaimed with anger: "My painter is no longer your adversary, it is I ; I will treat you as you treat him, and by the consideration you show I shall judge of the respect you have for your king. And further, know that I can raise seven peasants to the dignity of earl, but of seven earls I cannot make one Holbein."

The lord felt the force of the expression, and knowing that Henry was not joking, he promised him not only to stifle his vengeance, but even

---

(1) Plaindre se rend par *to pity;* se plaindre se dit *to complain.*

to become the protector of the painter.

Wolves.

There do not exist in all England either wolves or wild boars. It is to the reign of Edgar, in the tenth century that they trace the destruction of wolves in that country. That prince undertook a war of extermination against these ferocious animals, and succeeded in a short time, assisted by the nobles of the kingdom, in driving them into the mountains and forests of the country of Wales. At length when the Welsh came to acknowledge his sovereignty, he thought of attaching them more closely to his person by relieving them of a tribute which Athelstan had imposed on them, but in confiding to them the care of making war upon the wolves, and of delivering to him annually three hundred heads. In less than four years, it is said, the whole race of them was entirely destroyed.

They have often endeavoured to destroy them in France ; Charlemagne ordered all the governors of provinces to establish, under the title of wolf-hunters, men ordered to catch the wolves and to send him every year the skins of the wolves and cubs that they should have taken. The civil wars with which France was afflicted during the reign of Charles VI (the sixth) attracted a great number of these animals after the armies, and they became so formidable and so numerous that, after the famine which in 1438 (fourteen hundred and thirty-eight) caused the death of a great number of the inhabitants of Paris, they were seen in crowds penetrating the town; they devoured more than sixty persons there, and committed so many ravages, that the inhabitants were obliged to set a price upon their heads.

Since that time, war has been made upon them more or less according to the mischief they do; but in proportion as the population augments, and as towns and villages take the place of woods, those animals take refuge in the forests, whence they come out only when driven by hunger, or by the rigours of winter.

How the title of DAUPHIN, and that of PRINCE of WALES, belong to the eldest sons of the kings of France and England.

Andrew, the only son of Humbert, Prince of Dauphiny, perished in his infancy, by a very unfortunate event. His father, who loved him tenderly, was holding him one day in his arms, being at the window of a room in his castle, at the foot of which ran the Isère. Playing with the young prince, he slipped from his hands and fell into the river, where he was drowned. Humbert was so much afflicted by this accident, that he resolved from that moment to renounce the world, and to go and shut himself up in the solitude of a cloister. It was in consequence of this resolution that in 1343 (thirteen hundred and forty-three) he ceded his states to the prince Charles, then eight years of age, eldest son of the Duke of Normandy and grandson of Philip of Valois, to be transmitted successively to the eldest sons of the kings of France, with the title of Dauphin. Humbert received in exchange the sum of forty thousand francs, and a pension of ten thousand francs.

The eldest son of the King of England, since Edward I (the first), is styled prince of Wales. That king had long waged war against the inhabitants of that province, and although he had gained several brilliant victories, the Welsh still refused to acknowledge him for their sovereign, saying they would never submit to a foreign prince.

The cunning Edward, however, soon found means to conciliate them. His wife Eleanor being near her confinement, he conceived the idea of sending her to Caernarvon castle, in the principality of Wales, hoping to have a son born in that country. His desires were fulfilled, the queen brought forth a son on the 25th (twenty-fifth) of April, 1284 (twelve hundred and eighty-four).

Edward profited by that circumstance to ask of the Welsh if they would acknowledge for sovereign a prince their fellow-countryman. They replied that they would submit themselves to him, and would remain faithful. "Then", said the king, "I propose to you the prince my son, born in the midst of you in the castle of Caernarvon." Seeing that it would be a means of putting an end to the wars, which during so long a time had brought devastation into their country, the Welsh accepted the proposal of the king (*ou* the king's proposal), and from that time the eldest son of the King of England bears the title of Prince of Wales. In case of the death of the Prince of Wales, the title is given to his eldest son as heir-apparent to the crown. This important province is situated in the west of England, opposite Ireland.

Presence of Mind.

The caliph Hegiage, who by his cruelties was the horror of the people, was travelling as a spy through the provinces of his empire, without retinue, or mark of distinction. He meets with an Arab, and on the way says to him : " Friend, I should like to know what kind of man is this Hegiage of whom they speak so much. " — " Hegiage ", replies the Arab, " is not a man, he is a tiger, he is a monster." — " With what do they reproach him ?" — " With all species of crimes : he treats his subjects like dogs, he bathes in their blood ; but they will revenge themselves sooner or later."

" Thou hast doubtless seen him, since thou appearest to know him so well." — " No, never have I had the misfortune to meet so ferocious a beast." — " Well then! raise thine eyes (*ou* look up), it is to him that thou art speaking." The Arab, without manifesting the least surprise, looks at him stedfastly, and says boldly to him : " And you, do you know who I am?" — " No". — " I am of the family of Zobair, of which one of the descendants become mad one day in the year ; my day is to-day (*ou* this is my day)." Hegiage could not help admiring the presence of mind of the Arab, and said to him, on going away : " Thou art the most sensible (*ou* the wisest) madman that I have ever met."

A Palace of Ice.

During the winter of 1740 (seventeen hundred and forty) which was very long, and very severe, they constructed, upon the Neva, at St. Petersburg, a palace of ice. They took blocks of ice two or three feet in thickness; they shaped them, and carved ornaments upon them, and when they were placed they sprinkled them outside with coloured water which congealed immediately, and formed a remarkable variety. They made also six cannons and two mortars with their carriages, all in ice. They loaded them with ball, and fired them in presence of the whole court. The ball, at sixty paces, went through a plank two inches thick (*on* in thickness), and the cannon, which was but four inches thick, did not burst.

Another use of ice, which, at first sight, appears yet more extraordinary, is that which an English philosopher made in 1763 (seventeen hundred and sixty-three). He cut a piece of ice in the form of a lens nine feet nine inches in diameter, and five inches thick; he exposed it to the rays of the sun, and at seven feet distance he set fire to gunpowder, paper, and other combustible matter. One may therefore set fire to a powder-magazine with a piece of ice.

The Scotchman and the Americans.

A Scotch sergeant, who had been made prisoner by some wild Americans, perceiving that they were preparing to make him endure the greatest torments, thought of an ingenious method of escaping their cruelties. He said to them: "The fortune of war has placed me in your hands, and you intend to put me to a frightful death; but you deceive yourselves, for I possess the secret of rendering all your efforts impotent. Know, then, brave Americans, that in my country there are sages (*ou* wise men) who possess supernatural knowledge. One of them gave me, when I departed for the war, a charm which rendered me invulnerable. You have seen how I escaped from all your darts. Well, then, I will reveal that secret to you, on condition that you restore me to liberty when you are (1) convinced of its efficacy, by trials (*ou* experiments) that you may make upon me. Leave me only one hand at liberty, in order that I may rub myself with my magic powder."

The credulous Indians unbound one of the prisoner's arms. He immediately drew his snuff box from his pocket, and rubbed his neck with some of the powder, muttering a few

(1) Dans le style familier on met au présent le verbe qui suit *when*, quand. Voyez ma Grammaire pratique, p. 236.

words at the same time and making grotesque gestures.

He then said to the chief: "You, brave warrior, who hold my sabre, strike with all your might (*ou* strength), and you will see with your own eyes that, far from separating my head from my body, you will not even cut the skin of my neck."

The Indian chief, immediately draws the sabre, strikes, and sees the head of the Scotchman fall (*ou* roll) at some paces from him. — The astonished savages look at the dead body of the sergeant who had so well deceived them, admiring the trick he had employed to preserve himself from the torments of a long and cruel death.

A Kingdom lost through a private quarrel.

Earl Godwin, father of Queen Editha, the wife of Edward the Confessor, King of England, was dining one day with his sons Harold and Tostig at the king's table. Tostig, jealous of the preference which that prince showed to his brother, seized him by the hair and threw him to the ground : Harold soon rose, and fell upon Tostig with so much violence, that the king himself was obliged to interpose, in order to separate them. From that moment the two brothers became mortal enemies.

King Edward died a short time after this quarrel, having named (*ou* appointed) Harold to succeed him (*ou* as his successor). The new king soon learned that his brother was conspiring against him; he therefore exiled him. — Tostig, to revenge himself for that humiliation, went to visit William, duke of Normandy, who pretended to the throne of England : he even offered him his services. The duke confided some vessels to him, with which he went to Norway. There he obtained assistance of the king, Hardrada, and the two princes soon landed in England. Harold marched against them, and a sanguinary battle ensued. Hardrada and Tostig were killed, and victory declared for Harold; but in the midst of the rejoicings, he learns that William, Duke of Normandy, with a numerous army, has landed at Pevensey, in the county of Sussex, more than a hundred leagues from him and his forces.

Harold, although wounded in the last battle, hastened to march against the invaders : but he had not the time to well organise his army before giving battle. The combat took place at Senlac, the 13th (thirteenth) of October 1066 (one thousand and sixty-six); the fate of it remained a long time doubtful, and the carnage became horrible. At length Harold received an arrow in his (1) eye; he fell, and his death decided the fate of the battle, and of England. William seized the throne, and the Normans became masters of all the country.

---

(1) Pour les cas où l'article se traduit par l'adjectif possessif, voyez ma Grammaire pratique, p. 188.

Thus, in consequence of a quarrel between two brothers, the kingdom passed under the yoke of a foreign dynasty.

Duelling.

Gustavus-Adolphus, king of Sweden in 1611 (sixteen hundred and eleven), considered, like Louis XIV. (the fourteenth) private combats (*ou* duels) as the ruin of discipline. With the intention of abolishing this barbarous custom in his army, he had decreed the pain of death against all those who should fight a duel. Some time after, two superior officers who had some disputes, asked permission to settle their quarrel sword in hand.

Gustavus, although indignant at the proposal, consented to it; but he added that he would be a witness of the combat (*ou* fight), of which he appointed the time (*ou* hour) and the place. He went there with a corps (*ou* body) of infantry, which surrounded the two champions. He then called the executioner, and said to him : "The instant that one of these gentlemen is killed, cut off the head of the other in my presence." At these words, the two officers stood (*ou* remained) for some time motionless; at length they threw themselves at the king's feet, asked pardon of him (*ou* asked his pardon), and swore (*ou* vowed) eternal friendship to each other.

The Royal Poet and the Critic.

Louis XIV. (the fourteenth) amused himself sometimes in making (*ou* writing) verses. Having one day composed a little madrigal, which he himself did not think very good, he showed it to Marshal Grammont, saying to him : "Marshal, I beg of you to read these verses, and tell me if you have ever seen any so bad. Because it is known that I like poetry, they bring me all sorts of it." The marshal, after having read, said to the king : "Sire, your Majesty judges divinely well of all things; it is the most foolish and the most ridiculous madrigal that I have ever read."

The king laughed heartily, and said

to him : "Is it not true that he who composed it is a great coxcomb?" — "Sire, it is impossible to give him any other name (*ou* to call him anything else)." — "Well!" said the king, "I am delighted that you have spoken to me so frankly ; it is I who composed it." — "Ah ! sire, what treachery! may it please your Majesty to return it to me? I read it hastily." — "No, Marshal, the first sentiments are always the most natural."

The Children of Edward.

Edward IV. (the fourth), King of England, died in 1483 (fourteen hundred and eighty-three), leaving two sons ; the elder was only twelve years old, and the other was still younger by one year. Their uncle, the ambitious Richard, Duke of Gloucester, contrived by infamous intrigues to get himself chosen king, to the exclusion of young Edward, the heir to the crown. But the usurper soon learned that the friends of the young princes were conspiring to place Edward, the elder of the two brothers, on the throne of his father. He resolved to surmount that obstacle.

At first he endeavoured to induce the lieutenant of the Tower to find means of putting the young princes to death without any noise (*ou* disturbance); but the lieutenant frankly expressed to him the horror with which such a crime inspired him. Richard then sent to him an order to deliver the keys of the fortress, for twenty-four hours, to James Tyrrel, master of the horse. The same night, Tyrrel, accompanied by three villains, opened the door of the chamber where the two brothers were reposing, and the assassins smothered the poor children under the pillows, and buried them in a grave dug at the bottom of the staircase

---

The Children of Clodomir.

Clodomir, son of Clovis and king of Orleans, left, at his death, three children of tender age Being also deprived of their mother, the young orphans were brought up by Clotilda, wife of Clovis. Clotaire and Childebert, uncles of the princes, conceived the design of seizing upon the inheritance of their father; but dreading the firmness of Clotilda, they invited their nephews (1) to come to their court, under the pretext of putting them in possession of their father's kingdom. As soon as they arrived, Childebert shut them up in his palace, and sent to Clotilda a pair (2) of scissors and a poniard, to give her to understand that her grand-sons must choose between the cloister and death.

Clotilda, indignant at such perfidy, gave an answer worthy of the wife of Clovis: " I would rather ", said she, " that the dear children should cease

---

(1) Prononcez *névïouse.*

(2) Voyez Grammaire pratique, p. 27, note 4.

to live (*ou* should die) than see them degraded and deprived of their rights." The answer of Clotilda was the death-warrant of the young princes. Their uncles having had them brought into their presence, Clotaire seized the eldest, who was ten years old, and throwing him to the ground, plunged a poniard into his heart. At the sight of his murdered brother, the second, Gunthaire, throws himself at the feet of Childebert, and implores him, embracing his knees. The uncle appears touched; but Clotaire, reproaching him with his weakness, snatches the child and massacres him upon the body of his brother Theobald.

During this scene of horror, Clodoald, the youngest of the three brothers, had fled from the apartment.

A lord of the court concealed him for some time, and afterwards made him enter a cloister. After having passed some years there, Clodoald built, in the woods near Paris, a hermitage, where he founded a monastery, and terminated his existence in that retreat about the year 560 (five hundred and sixty). After his death, Clodoald became celebrated, and was canonized. His great renown drew (*ou* attracted) a crowd of pilgrims, which contributed to populate and enrich that place, to which they gave the name of Sanctus Clodoaldus, which afterwards, by corruption, was changed to that of Saint-Cloud. The church honours his memory on the 7th (seventh) of September.

An Episode of Saint Bartholomew.

Among the victims of this horrible day was a child, with his father and elder brother. The two latter fell dead under the poniards of the assassins; the child, wounded also, falls on the dead bodies of his relations, and the murderers go away. Some wretches come afterwards to plunder the corpses; and one of them, seeing the little boy, said : " Alas! it is a great pity; what could this child have done?"

At these words, the child, who was still alive, raises his head slowly, and says softly : " I am not dead. " — " Do not stir, my poor little fellow, have patience, " said the man, who was touched with compassion ; and when he saw that no one was near them, he asked him who he was, and where he wished to go. I am related to (*ou* a relation of) the grand master of the artillery, replied the child ; take me to the Arsenal, you will be well rewarded."

The man, who was a marker at a tennis-court, named Verdelet, took him by the hand and, meeting at some distance somebody who asked him who the little boy was, he replied: "It is my nephew, who has been getting tipsy and fighting with his companions ; I am taking him home to give him a whipping (*ou* flogging)."

At length, by thus using precaution, Verdelet arrives with his charge at the Arsenal ; he delivers him into the hands of Marshal Biron, who rewards him generously. James Nompar de Caumont (such was the name of the child), having thus escaped from that frightful carnage, became duke of La Force, and lived to the age of eighty years.

The Emperor's Calves.

One evening, at Malmaison, Napoleon was in private conversation with Josephine, in the little blue drawing-room; he calls, and asks for a cup of tea. The page on duty brings one ready prepared, upon a silver-gilt waiter. Wishing to spare the emperor the trouble of rising to take it, he approaches too carelessly, the point of his foot becomes entangled in a fold of the carpet, he loses his balance, and spills the scalding tea upon the legs of the emperor, who, that evening, had no boots on.

Napoleon drew back his chair with signs of pain, which he expressed energetically. "My God! Bonaparte", said Josephine laughing, "how you swear lately, what a vile habit!" — "But", replies the emperor, wiping his stockings with his handkerchief, "that little rascal there has scalded my calves in a horrible manner." Fortunately the cup, although of delicate porcelain, was not broken. Napoleon, who picked it up himself, made the remark; Josephine then said to him, laughing still more loudly, "Come, come, Bonaparte, don't be angry, there is but little harm."

Benevolence.

The Count de Saurai, Archbishop of Bordeaux, was the almoner of the poor; his purse belonged to them more than to himself. "My lord", said a person to him one day, "a poor woman is come to implore your charity; what will you do for her?" — "How old is she?" — "Seventy years." — "Is she very miserable?" — "She says so." — "We must believe her; give her twenty-five francs." — "Twenty-five francs! my lord, the sum is too large, and besides, she is a Jewess." — "A Jewess, good God!" — "Yes, my lord." — "Oh, that is very different; then give her fifty francs, and thank her for her visit."

The charitable archbishop paid so little attention to his own wants that his wardrobe was often very scantily supplied. One day, a sister of charity, who took care of his linen, came and related to him a lamentable story of a poor man who was in want of shirts and sheets She obtains wherewith to buy some, and runs immediately to employ the money in ordering sheets and shirts for himself. He laughed very much when he learned the pious fraud employed by the good sister.

By Means of Boots *ou* **Through Boots.**

Napoleon, after the siege of Toulon, having fallen into disgrace with the national convention, solicited, it is said, permission to quit the service of France (*ou* the French service) and go to Turkey, where they were preparing an armament against Austria. Fréron, however, a deputy of the convention, succeeded in obtaining for him the command of the artillery in Holland. They had allowed him fifteen days to go to his post; but a singular event prevented his journey. Napoleon had ordered several pairs of boots; the boot-maker brings them home on the eve of his departure, and presents him his bill.

Napoleon's purse not being very well furnished, he wishes to give the boot-maker a draft upon the minister at war. The boot-maker refuses, and Napoleon, out of patience, refuses in his turn to take the boots. It becomes necessary to order some others. Instead of setting off on the 4th (fourth) of Vendémiaire, Napoleon decides upon waiting some days longer. During this delay he receives a word from Barras, a deputy of the convention, and chief of the forces, recommending him not to depart, because something important was preparing. It was nothing less than a new revolution. It broke out on the 13th (thirteenth) of Vendémiaire, the 5th (fifth) of October. We know that the part which Napoleon played on that day entirely changed his position and his fortune, and it was afterwards said that Napoleon had become emperor by means of boots (*ou* by boots).

The Love of Work Renders the Heart Sensitive.

The celebrated Florian showed very early the happiest disposition for study, and consequently made rapid progress (1). In his rural walks, he one day entered the cottage of an unfortunate day-labourer whom he found in the greatest distress. He drew out his purse, gave the contents of it to the poor man, and promised to return. He kept his word, and carried to him continually his pocket-money. His father was not long in perceiving that his money disappeared quickly. He wished to

(1) *Progrès* n'a pas de pluriel en anglais.

ascertain the use he made of it, and determined to follow him.

The child sets off as usual, and goes directly to the cottage. The father follows him, approaches, and sees him put into the hand of the labourer the little sum that he had just received for his week. Unable to contain the joy which this trait of humanity causes him, he shows himself, and embraces his dear son, bathing him with tears of affection.

Thus passed the youth of Florian, in doing good, and in cultivating his mind by a constant application to the study of literature. On the 14th (fourteenth) of May, 1788 (seventeen hundred and eighty-eight), he was elected member of the French Academy. We will here cite a paragraph from his speech at his reception.

"If the love of work renders us happy at all ages (*ou* at every age), it is above all useful in youth. It is when the unruly passions struggle incessantly against feeble reason; when the heart, without defence, open, it may be said, on all sides (*ou* on every side), offers itself to all kinds of seductions; when the mind, hungering after new emotions, flies to meet every thing which may affect it: it is then that it is necessary to provide occupation for that restless activity, to direct towards a useful end that ardour of which one should avail oneself, and to save one's life from ennui, which is often the forerunner of vice."

The Snuff-Box.

General Count *** being at a coffee-house with some friends, felt for (*ou* sought for) his snuff-box, which he had used a few moments before. Not finding it, he calls for the master of the house. The latter immediately closes the doors, and begs the persons who were present to turn out their pockets. An old officer, retired in a corner, was the only one who refused. He even went so far as to draw his sword, and threatened to stab the first who should approach to search him. The general, enraged at this resistance, also draws his sword; but the movement makes him feel something hard which struck his leg : it was the snuff-box, which had fallen to the bottom of his coat, through a hole in his pocket. He makes his apologies (*ou* he apologises) to the company, and taking the officer aside, asks him the cause of his refusal.

"Sir", answers the unknown, "I would rather have died than have exposed my shame to the eyes of the world. I have spent my fortune and worn out my strength in the king's service. The revolution has deprived me of everything; my present means allow me only two slight meals a day : I have one of them at this moment in my pocket, it consists only of a small loaf (*ou* roll) and a piece of cheese, which one of the waiters of the coffee-house, the only confidant of my misery, procures me every day. I leave you to judge, sir, of the motives of my refusal." The general, moved by so touching a representation, offered his table to his respectable companion in arms, and did not delay procuring for him, by his influence, a pension which placed him above necessity.

The Ass Ennobled.

On the day of the corouation of Napoleon, the departure of the pope from the Tuileries experienced rather a long delay, in consequence of an unforeseen obstacle. At Rome, when the Holy Father left his palace to go and officiate in any church, one of his chamberlains used to set off before him mounted upon an ass, carrying a large processional cross. It was at the very moment when his holiness was going out, that M. de Segur was informed of that custom. The chamberlain having refused to take a horse, or even a mule, they were obliged to send all the grooms of the stables in search of an ass. They had the good fortune to find one sufficiently presentable at a fruiterer's (*ou* fruitwoman's). They hastened to have it curried, and to cover it with a housing of very rich velvet, ornamented with tassels which hung down to the ground, and to bring it to the foot of the grand staircase of the pavilion of Flora.

The susceptible chamberlain mounted it, and, armed with his great cross, which he carried as a knight carries his lance, he proceeded alone with immovable *sang-froid*, through the double rank of soldiers who lined the quays, and who, less devout than the soldiers of the pope, could not help laughing at this spectacle, the more extraordinary as the ass was of small size, while his (*ou* its) rider had excessively long legs.

The Postmaster.

M. de Lavalette, director of the general post under the empire, was condemned to death for treason after the fall of Napoleon. It is known that on the eve of the day fixed for the execution, his wife devoted herself to save the life of her husband, and succeeded in procuring his escape, by changing clothes with him. By the aid of (*ou* aided by) three officers of the English army, he quitted Paris disguised as an English general. On arriving at the last post house in France, he was recognized by the post-master who, approaching the carriage, said to him : " Have you heard speak of the escape of Lavalette? I should much like to know if he is out of Paris." M. de Lavalette, who thinks himself betrayed, replies, stammering, and with the English accent : "Me not know; to be officer English, running post for my government on Brussels. —Well, replies the post-master, lowering his voice, since you are going to Brussels, do me the pleasure to take charge of these hundred napoleons that I owe him; I hope you will find him there; deliver them to him from me."

In such moments one fears to express one's gratitude, and although M. de Lavalette had to do with a man whose fortune he had made, he was obliged to refuse coldly; while concealing the tears of affection which bathed his eyes; but, on arriving at the frontier, he said to the postilion who drove him: "Here, my friend; here are ten napoleons to drink to thy master's health, thou wilt tell him that Lavalette is saved."

THE END.

TABLE DES MATIÈRES

PREMIÈRE SECTION

Règles et applications.

DEUXIÈME SECTION

Développement général de la première section.

TROISIÈME SECTION

Anecdotes historiques.

Paris. Typ. A. Hennuyer, rue Darcet, 7.

LIBRAIRIE FRANÇAISE ET ANGLAISE DE J.-H. TRUCHY
CH. LEROY, SUCCESSEUR
26, BOULEVARD DES ITALIENS, PARIS

OUVRAGES ÉLÉMENTAIRES

POUR L'ÉTUDE

DE LA LANGUE ANGLAISE

**DIALOGUES, GRAMMAIRES, LIVRES DE TRADUCTIONS
DICTIONNAIRES, CORRESPONDANCES
LIVRES AVEC PRONONCIATION FIGURÉE
TRADUCTIONS INTERLINÉAIRES
OUVRAGES ANGLAIS ET FRANÇAIS EN REGARD**

Ouvrages par M. Sadler, Cours gradué de langue anglaise à l'usage des classes élémentaires, divisé en quatre parties.

SADLER. **Cours gradué de langue anglaise** (1re partie), ou MANUEL DE PHRASES FRANÇAISES ET ANGLAISES, contenant de nombreux Vocabulaires français et anglais des mots les plus usités, suivis chacun de petites phrases élémentaires leur servant d'exercices, accompagnés de Dialogues familiers, à l'usage des classes élémentaires. 29e édition, 1 vol. in-18 cartonné, dos en toile. 1 fr. 50

SADLER. **Cours gradué de langue anglaise** (2e partie), ou PETIT COURS DE VERSIONS à l'usage des classes élémentaires, contenant un recueil d'Anecdotes, de traits instructifs et amusants, etc., suivi d'un *Dictionnaire anglais-français* de tous les mots qui se trouvent dans l'ouvrage. 26e édition, 1 vol. in-18 cartonné, dos en toile. 2 fr.

SADLER. **Cours gradué de langue anglaise** (3e partie), ou PETIT COURS DE THÈMES à l'usage des classes élémentaires, suivi d'un *Dictionnaire français-anglais* de tous les mots qui se trouvent dans l'ouvrage. 11e édition, 1 vol. in-18 cartonné. 2 fr.

SADLER. **Cours gradué de langue anglaise** (4e partie), ou CORRIGÉ DU PETIT COURS DE THÈMES à l'usage des classes élémentaires (traduction des thèmes et anecdotes contenus dans le cours gradué, 3e partie). 1 vol. in-18 cart., dos en toile. 1 fr. 50

Ce cours gradué de langue anglaise, divisé en quatre parties, est devenu d'un usage presque général dans toutes les *classes* élémentaires.

Le Petit Maître d'anglais, ou PREMIERS ÉLÉMENTS DE LA LANGUE ANGLAISE, mis à la portée de la jeunesse ; accompagnés d'exercices courts et faciles, propres à faire l'application des règles précises qui y sont développées ; par J. STEPHENS. Approuvé par le Conseil de l'instruction publique. 5e édition, 1 vol. in-18 cartonné. 1 fr. 50

SADLER. **Grammaire pratique de la langue anglaise,** ou MÉTHODE FACILE POUR APPRENDRE CETTE LANGUE ; contenant une dissertation détaillée sur l'emploi de *shall, will, do*, etc. ; contenant aussi un tableau colorié, donnant la valeur figurative des principales prépositions *to, at, over, from, of, into, in*. 23e édition, 1 vol. in-12 cartonné. 2 fr. 50

SADLER. **Exercices anglais,** ou COURS DE THÈMES GRADUÉS, pour servir de développements aux règles de la *Grammaire anglaise*. Les difficultés de la traduction du français en anglais y sont présentées graduellement et aplanies par des notes grammaticales mises au bas des pages, ou avec des renvois aux règles énoncées dans la grammaire. 20e édition, 1 vol. in-12 cartonné. 3 fr.

SADLER. **Corrigé des exercices anglais,** ou TRADUCTION EXACTE DES THÈMES GRADUÉS ; ouvrage par le moyen duquel on peut se corriger soi-même. Nouvelle édition, 1 vol. in-12 cartonné. 2 fr. 50

On ne saurait trop recommander ces trois ouvrages, ainsi que le suivant, qui forment en quelque sorte un *Cours complet d'Anglais supérieur*, adopté par les principales maisons d'éducation.

SADLER. **Cours de versions anglaises,** ou RECUEIL CHOISI DE TRAITS HISTORIQUES, extraits divers en prose, etc.; suivis des morceaux les plus brillants de la poésie anglaise, par Moore, Byron, W. Scott, etc., etc.; avec *notes explicatives* en français, pour éclaircir les difficultés qui se rencontrent dans le texte. 11e édition, in-12 cartonné. 4 fr.

SADLER. **Manuel classique de conversations françaises et anglaises,** divisé en trois parties: 1° *Choix de dialogues* anglais et français, sur toutes les circonstances particulières de la vie; 2° *Recueil de locutions* et d'expressions, dans lesquelles les étrangers sont exposés à des contresens; 3° *Riche Vocabulaire* de tous les mots les plus usités, classés par matière, suivi de tables comparatives des poids, mesures et monnaies, etc., des deux pays. 9e édition, 1 fort vol. in-18 cartonné, dos en toile (800 pages). (*Adopté par le Conseil de l'instruction publique.*) 3 fr.

Cours d'anglais, professé à l'École communale supérieure de Paris, par P. SADLER, publié sous la direction de MM. Goubaux, chef de l'école, et Lamé, professeur de physique à l'École polytechnique.

PREMIÈRE ANNÉE.

Manuel d'Anglais, 1re partie. Grammaire et Thèmes, suivis d'un Dictionnaire Français-Anglais. 1 vol. in-12 cart. 1 fr. 25

Manuel d'Anglais, 2e partie. Versions et Dialogues, suivis d'un Dictionnaire Anglais-Français. 1 vol. in-12 cartonné. 1 fr. 25

DEUXIÈME ANNÉE.

Manuel d'Anglais, 3e partie. Thèmes et Syntaxe, contenant

un choix de morceaux français à traduire en anglais, et suivis d'un précis de la Syntaxe anglaise. 1 vol. in-12 cart. 1 fr. 25

Manuel d'Anglais, 4e partie. Versions, contenant un choix de morceaux anglais, extraits historiques, etc., tirés des auteurs anglais, etc. 1 vol. in-12 cartonné. 1 fr. 25

TROISIÈME ANNÉE.

Manuel d'Anglais, 5e partie. Leçons de littérature française, Prose et Vers, ou Extraits d'auteurs français, à traduire en anglais. 1 vol. in-12 cartonné. 1 fr. 25

Manuel d'Anglais, 6e partie. Leçons de Littérature anglaise, Prose et Vers, ou Extraits d'auteurs anglais à traduire en français, 1 vol. in-12 cartonné. 1 fr. 25

SADLER. **Nouveau Dictionnaire portatif anglais-français et français-anglais,** renfermant, outre un très grand nombre de mots qui ne se trouvent pas dans les autres dictionnaires : Un appendice contenant un Dictionnaire anglais-français et français-anglais des principaux TERMES TECHNIQUES ayant rapport aux Sciences et aux Arts, à la Marine, à l'Art militaire, à la Mécanique, aux Machines locomotives, Chemins de fer, Bateaux à vapeur, à la Chimie, à la Physique, à l'Astronomie, aux Métiers, entièrement inédit; un Dictionnaire géographique, une Liste des noms de baptême, etc., par P. SADLER. Deux tomes en un volume, nouvelle édition, augmentée de la prononciation anglaise figurée par des sons français. Broché. 6 fr. Reliure anglaise en toile. 7 fr.

SADLER'S. **Classical History of England,** from the first Roman invasion to the present time (1874), with Questions for examination (for the use of Schools). 1 vol. in-12 (576 pages). 3 fr. 50

SADLER. **The Poetical Preceptor,** divisé en deux parties : 1re partie, *Traité théorique et pratique de prosodie anglaise,* dans lequel on fait connaître la structure et la composition des vers anglais ; 2e partie, *Choix des meilleurs poètes anglais de toutes les époques.* 1 vol. in-12 (500 pages). 4 fr. 50

ON VEND SÉPARÉMENT :

SADLER. **Theoretical and practical Treatise of English prosody.** 1 vol. in-12. 2fr. 50

SADLER. **Selection from the most celebrated British poets,** elegant extracts in Poetry from Addison, Byron, Chaucer, Cowper, Campbell, Goldsmith, Milton, Moore, Pope, Shakspeare, Southey, W. Scott, Thomson, etc. 1 vol. in-12. 3 fr. 50

SADLER. **L'Art de la correspondance anglaise et française,** ou RECUEIL DE LETTRES EN ANGLAIS ET EN FRANÇAIS sur toutes sortes de sujets familiers; suivi d'un choix des meilleurs épistolaires anglais, de modèles de lettres commerciales, d'un vocabulaire des termes de commerce, etc. 7e édition, contenant des améliorations très importantes. 2 vol. in-12 brochés. 6 fr.

SADLER'S. **Art of English Correspondence,** being a collection of familiar letters selected from the best English writers, models of commercial letters, etc., etc., by P. SADLER. 5e édition, 1 vol. in-12 broché (*le texte anglais seulement*). 3 fr. 50

AUTRES OUVRAGES

POUR L'ÉTUDE DE LA LANGUE ANGLAISE.

STEBBING. **Nouvelle Méthode pratique de langue anglaise,** renfermant des *exercices simplifiés* sur les règles de la grammaire, suivie d'un dictionnaire anglais-français de tous les mots employés dans l'ouvrage, avec *prononciation figurée*. 3e éd., 1 vol. in-18 jésus, cart., dos en toile. 1 fr. 80

BENSLEY. **A garland of entertaining Anecdotes,** for the use of french students of the English Language, with explanatory notes in French. (Choix d'anecdotes en anglais avec *notes explicatives en français*.) 1 vol. in-18, beaux caractères, cartonné, dos en toile. 2 fr. 50

JOHNSON. **Versions anglaises,** contenant : 1° Exercices pratiques et prononciation figurée ; 2° Texte anglais avec prononciation chiffrée et traduction interlinéaire ; 3° Texte anglais avec prononciation chiffrée et traduction en regard ; 4° Extraits de littérature anglaise ; 5° Choix de poésies, versification anglaise. 8e édition. (*Approuvé par l'Université.*) 1 vol. in-12, broché. 3 fr. 50

JOHNSON. **Etudes progressives de la langue anglaise.** Exercices préliminaires sur l'application pratique de la méthode Johnson, Extraits interlinéaires, Morceaux choisis, Abrégé de la grammaire anglaise, Dialogues français et anglais, etc. 1 vol. in-12, broché. 2 fr. 50

FLEMING et TIBBINS. **Stepping-stone to english,** ou MANUEL ANGLAIS DU JEUNE FRANÇAIS. Première partie : contenant des exercices (en anglais) sur toutes les parties de la grammaire anglaise, en une série de phrases pratiques et usuelles. (*Adopté par l'Université.*) 2e édition, 1 vol. in-18, cartonné. 2 fr. 50

FLEMING. **English verbs and english prepositions;** rationale of the People's english, or specimens of the free and easy. (*L'Anglais raisonné.*) Travail entièrement neuf sur les verbes anglais modifiés par des prépositions (*à l'usage des lycées*), par C. FLEMING, professeur d'anglais au lycée Bonaparte. 1 vol. in-12, broché. 3 fr.

Cet ouvrage, dont le travail n'avait jamais été publié jusqu'à ce jour, offre des exercices (en anglais) de traduction sur toutes les phrases où il entre des prépositions anglaises qui rendent souvent la traduction presque impossible.

FLEMING. **Coup d'œil rapide sur le subjonctif anglais,** précédé de quelques remarques sur l'anglais et la grammaire anglaise. 1 vol. in-8. 3 fr. 50

MALLARMÉ. **Les Mots anglais.** Petite philologie

à l'usage des classes et du monde. 1 vol. in-12, cartonné. 3 fr. 50

Ce livre est le premier en France qui étudie l'anglais au point de vue scientifique moderne ; et cependant, s'il peut satisfaire le goût nouveau du Public pour les recherches philologiques, sa méthode, claire et copiée sur l'Histoire, est surtout faite pour aider à la jeunesse studieuse des lycées et des maisons d'éducation.

Trois parties, outre une introduction historique et la conclusion, composent l'ouvrage, neuves chacune autant que le plan ; celle-ci groupe en familles, d'après les radicaux, tous les vocables originels ; celle-là étudie les lois qui ont présidé à la transformation, dans le nom et le sens, des vieux mots français devenus anglais. La dernière rapporte aux langues classiques les termes faussement attribués au français, tout en revendiquant pour nous la plupart des règles de la dérivation : elle n'est pas la moins riche en surprises.

A la faveur de cette *Clef du Dictionnaire*, le labeur si pénible d'ordinaire imposé à la mémoire par l'étude d'un idiome, devient un jeu pour l'intelligence.

Pareil traité, *les Mots anglais*, s'adresse donc à quiconque chez nous s'adonne au parler d'outre-Manche : il intéresse même les Anglais en leur offrant maint détail qu'on ne trouve dans aucun des manuels spéciaux publiés en Angleterre; et tout Français désireux, soit de connaître à fond sa langue propre, soit de suivre à l'étranger les transformations d'un grand nombre de mots d'ici, oubliés, et qui ne se survivent que là.

The Vicar of Wakefield, A tale by Oliver Goldsmith, nouvelle édition avec de nombreuses notes explicatives, par W.-A. MORGAN, ancien professeur au lycée Saint-Louis. (*Edition classique.*) 1 vol. in-18, broché. 1 fr. 50

An Essay on Man, in four epistles, by Alexander POPE ; **the Traveller, the deserted Village**, by Oliver GOLDSMITH. 1 vol. in-18. 1 fr. 50

BYRON'S (Lord). **Select poetical Works**, containing : the Corsair, a tale ; — Lara, a tale ; — the Giaour, a tale ; — the Bride of Abydos, — the Siege of Corinth, — the Prisoner of Chillon, — Select Poems. 1 vol. in-12 (376 pages). 4 fr.

On a réuni dans ce volume toutes les plus jolies compositions poétiques de lord Byron, en ayant le soin d'en faire un recueil qui puisse être mis sans hésitation dans les mains de tout le monde.

TRUCHY'S EDITION
OF
ENGLISH PLAYS
WITH EXPLANATORY FRENCH NOTES

The School for Scandal, a comedy in five acts, by SHERIDAN; with a biographical sketch, critical notice, and, for the first time, explanatory french notes, by J. SHORT. 1 v. in-18. Fourth edit. 1 fr.

Cette édition du chef-d'œuvre de l'art dramatique en Angleterre contient des notes explicatives en français pour les idiotismes et les mots inusités qui s'y trouvent; elle a été choisie et adoptée dans tous les cours d'anglais.

The Rivals, a comedy in five acts, by SHERIDAN, improved with explanatory french notes, by SHORT. 1 vol. in-18. Third edition. 1 fr.

The School for Scandal avait besoin d'un pendant aussi remarquable que *The Rivals* du même auteur. Cette édition se fait remarquer par la correction du texte et les notes explicatives placées au bas de chaque page pour donner la signification des mots les plus difficiles, leurs synonymes, leurs étymologies, etc.

She Stoops to Conquer, a comedy in five acts, by Ol. GOLDSMITH; to which are added biographical and critical remarks, besides numerous notes in french, philological observations, a vocabulary of difficult words, a glossary, etc., etc., by J. SHORT. 1 vol. in-18. 1 fr.

Raising the wind, a Play in two acts, by J. KENNEY, with biographical and critical remarks; a new edition improved with explanatory french notes, by Ad. BROWN. 1 vol. in-18. 1 fr.

The Lady of Lyons, a drama in five acts, by E. L. BULWER, to which are added *The Wife, the Daughter*, two plays by KNOWLES. 1 fort vol. in-18. 3 fr. 50

Paris. — T

www.ingramcontent.com/pod-product-compliance
Ingram Content Group UK Ltd.
Pitfield, Milton Keynes, MK11 3LW, UK
UKHW021055230726
13926UKWH00004B/1868

9 782013 630542